## ABOUT THE BOOK

"Overall, the book has many uses . . . it capsulizes the life and significance of eight modern Catholic Christians in a way that makes them easily accessible."

—*The Church World*

"Eight 'saints' are profiled in this fascinating religious book, each presented by a different author. Great care was taken in the selection of subjects and the gifted writers who describe their early lives and later accomplishments, making this a valuable modern commentary."

—*Los Angeles Times*

"Delaney has rallied a stellar array of eight recognized authors to eulogize these real-life examples of the many saintly men and women who live today and who do God's work as courageously and quietly as the saints of the past."

—*Today's Parish*

"The biographees . . . represent a range of backgrounds and situations . . . Readable and appropriate for popular collections."

—*Library Journal*

". . . a spirited and engaging collection."

—*The Catholic Weekly*

# SAINTS
# ARE NOW

John J. Delaney,
editor

# SAINTS ARE NOW

Eight Portraits
of Modern Sanctity

(Complete and unabridged)

IMAGE BOOKS
A Division of Doubleday & Company, Inc.
Garden City, New York
1983

Image Book edition published March 1983 by special arrangement with Doubleday & Company, Inc.

The poem "In No Strange Land" is reprinted by permission of Hawthorn Properties, Elsvier-Dutton Publishing Co., Inc. From the book *The Kingdom of God* by Francis Thompson. Copyright 1923, 1951.

*Library of Congress Cataloging in Publication Data*
Main entry under title:
Saints are now.
Contents: Dorothy Day/Willaim D. Miller—
Pope John XXIII/Gary MacEoin—John
LaFarge/Edward S. Stanton—[etc.]
1. Catholics—Biography.  I. Delaney,
John J.
BX4669.S25   1983      282'.092'2 [B]
ISBN 0-385-17356-3 (pbk.)     AACR2
Library of Congress Catalog Card Number 82-458661

*This book is dedicated to these friends
of so many years in grateful apprecia-
tion of that most precious of gifts—
their friendship.
Ann—as always
Clair and Danny
Lillian and Henry
Neal
Peggy and Joe
Mildred, Margaret and Tommy
Virginia and Sal
Joan and Harold*

# *CONTENTS*

# INTRODUCTION

Several years ago a national news magazine devoted its
front cover to the major story: Where are our heroes?
In the inaugural address Ronald Reagan delivered after
he was sworn in as fortieth President of the United
States, he replied: "Those who say we are in a time
when there are no heroes just don't know where to
look." And what he said about heroes applies with
equal force to saints.

It is the firm conviction of this author and the thesis
of this book that the saints are very much with us
today. Unlike the President's heroes, it is not so much a
question of where to look to find saints; rather it is
merely the need to remove the blinders from our eyes,
for saints are here in our age just as they have been in
every age for the past two millennia. Men and women
living saintly lives are laboring among us, large as life
and some larger than life, doing God's work as saints
have done through the centuries and will continue to
do in the centuries ahead.

One of the reasons for the myopic vision we display
in regard to saints is that too many of us have, often
subconsciously, accepted the premise that saints are of
the past. They were a breed of men and women whose
works and reported wonders were uncritically accepted
in past eras of less sophistication and more credulity
than our own. Far too often, the obvious distortions
and exaggerations of the deeds, activities, and often

unbelievable and purposeless miracles attributed by fiercely partisan adherents to many we have been taught were saints have contributed to the belief that saints are a relic of a time when men and women uncritically accepted as fact much that today would be considered merely feats of the imagination. If this uncritical acceptance of hearsay and exaggeration is typical of ages past (and I say "if" for I seriously question this stereotyping of ages other than our own), then have we not in our times swung to the other extreme where we question everything, believe in nothing and yet revel in the rumors, innuendoes and half-truths that are the stock in trade of the scandal mongers whose gossip results in the wholesale destruction of the reputation of any man or woman who rises to any prominence?

The time has come when this contemporary approach to saintly figures should be recognized for the same distortion of which we accuse other ages. Modern scientific discoveries have emphasized that the great myths of antiquity were not simply products of someone's imagination; they had a basis in fact (one recalls the dramatic discovery of the real city of Troy by Heinrich Schliemann from evidence he found in the *Iliad* and the *Odyssey*, a city that for centuries had been regarded by the experts as existing only in fantasy). Similarly, archaeological discoveries have confirmed as fact many incidents, places, and figures in the Bible that sceptics had derided as imaginary. And so it is time we once again consider the legends of the saints and the concept of sainthood as based on reality, and give them the same unbiased consideration we so readily accord other persons and incidents and institutions from the past.

In order to decide whether the concept of sainthood is still valid today we should examine briefly, however inadequately in such brief compass (for books can be and have been written on the subject), the question of what is a saint.

It seems to me the very essence of sainthood is outlined in Jesus's own words and command in Matthew: "But when the Pharisees heard that he had silenced the Sadducees, they got together and to disconcert him, one of them put a question, 'Master, which is the greatest commandment of the Law?' Jesus said, *You must love the Lord your God with all your heart, with all your soul, and with all your mind.* This is the greatest and the first commandment. The second resembles it: *You must love your neighbor as yourself.* On these two commandments hang the whole Law and the Prophets also'" (Matthew 22:34–40). It is a simple enough statement, but living its precepts—ah! that is another matter. To me the unquenchable determination and the unceasing effort to live to the hilt Christ's ideal as expressed above is the way to sainthood. How well one is able to live up to Jesus's dictum is the measure of sainthood.

And it is obeying both aspects of Christ's command that distinguishes the saint from the secular humanitarian. Note that he designated loving the Lord your God as the first and greatest commandment. There can be no love of neighbor that is not accompanied by love of God, and the two loves cannot be separated. The first letter of John, in forceful language allowing no compromise, is emphatic on this point: "Anyone who says, 'I love God,' and hates his brother, is a liar, since a man who does not love his brother that he can see cannot love God whom he has never seen. So this is the commandment that he has given us, that anyone who loves God must also love his brother" (4:20–21). Intrinsic, then, to any saintly life is adherence to these two fundamental commandments.

From these two commandments of the Lord flow two corollaries. The first of these is complete abandonment of self to God—proclaimed by all saints as indispensable in the pursuit of spiritual perfection. As Brother Lawrence of the Resurrection put it in his spiritual classic *The Practice of the Presence of God* (Garden City, New York: Image Books, 1977), "We must trust God once and for all and abandon ourselves to Him alone"; and on entering the religious life, he "resolved to give myself entirely to God. . . ." No matter how onerous the burdens placed on us, no matter what pains and sufferings we are called to endure, he says, they are gifts from God who will give us the wherewithal to endure them if we but believe and put "all our trust in Him." This the saints understood and understand as do all who would follow in their footsteps.

The second corollary is complete dedication to one's fellow man. Whether practiced by a Francis of Assisi in the humblest of circumstances or by a pope or ruler in the pomp and circumstance of the papacy or a royal court (after all, is not the pope the servant of the servants of God?), it behooves all of us to heed Christ's command repeated over and over again in the New Testament, "You must love your neighbor as yourself" (Matthew 19:19; Mark 12:31, 33; Romans 13:9; Galatians 5:14; James 2:8). This, too, the saints understood, accepted unreservedly, and practiced, each in his or her individual way.

And so it seems to me how perfectly a man or woman follows these precepts and puts them into practice determines whether or not that person is a saint. One thing is certain—no one can be a saint who does not practice the admonitions of the Lord stated above.

In passing I cannot resist noting that this attitude is in direct contradiction of the "Me" philosophy so prevalent in the sixties which emphasized self and "my way" as the most important things in life and never mind the other person. In time I suspect that era and its philosophy will be recognized for the wasteland it

was, and not least of the causes for this judgment will
be the philosophy so prevalent that categorically con-
troverted Christ's two great commandments.

Which brings me to the eight men and women I
have selected for inclusion in this volume. Let me
emphasize I am not canonizing them. There is a formal
process for canonization that has been established by
the Church which decides who is worthy to be declared a saint. But in the final analysis it is God who
makes ultimate decisions. The Church is entrusted with
the task of publicly proclaiming sainthood. But just as
a pope can create a cardinal *in pectore* so I am convinced God recognizes many as saints who are not
publicly proclaimed. After all, saints have been canonized centuries after their deaths, but surely they were
no less saints before their formal canonization than
after the ceremonies publicly proclaiming that fact.
Further, the Church celebrates All Saints Day on
which she honors *all* saints, not only those who have
been formally canonized.

In the case of the eight men and women I have included, I merely offer them as possible candidates for
sainthood and leave it to you the reader and the formal
judgment of the Church to decide if they are worthy of
being called saints. I will discuss more specifically the
reasons that caused me to include them in this volume,
but at this time I would merely point out that all of
them to the best of their abilities and in their own diverse ways meet the criteria I have established above.

Two further generalizations about them. As is true of
all saints, all of these eight men and women are human
beings and possess not only traits associated with holiness but also baser human qualities. But the crux of the
matter is not that they possessed and exhibited these
human weaknesses but that they fought and overcame
their human frailties on their path to God. Their very
humanness is part of the essence of all saints. Thomas

Merton struck to the heart of the matter in *Seeds of Contemplation* (Norwalk, Conn.: New Directions, 1949) when he said, "Before you can be a saint, you have got to be human."

A second generalization is that saints do not become saints after their deaths. In a magnificent public television documentary on Mother Teresa, "The World of Mother Teresa," a British doctor devoting himself to helping her in caring for the sick commented, "When she is dead, she'll be a saint." I completely disagree with his remark. Saints are made not in death but during their lifetimes by the lives they lead. Recognition of their sainthood often comes after their deaths, but the elements of that sainthood are forged by their deeds and activities during their lifetimes. Not infrequently in the past recognition of this fact has caused certain men and women to be proclaimed saints during their lifetimes by their fellows. Indeed, in the long history of the Church the formal canonization procedure now in effect is a relatively new process and accounts for a small percentage of those we now call saints. Most saints were created by those who recognized their sanctity and the holiness of their lives and proclaimed that fact.

Which brings us to the specific reasons for selecting the men and women included in this volume.

First was the fact that they lived and performed their deeds during the lifetime of most of the readers of this book. One of them is still alive, one died in 1980, and with one exception (Edith Stein, who died in 1942) all lived well into the second half of the twentieth century. These are not men and women of past centuries; they are of now. Millions have met them or seen them on television or read about them in contemporary newspapers and magazines. They are men and women of the twentieth century confronted with the problems and perils of the atomic age just as you and I.

They did not wrestle with obscure problems of a time and age when practices and customs were different from ours and strange to us. They are our fellow men and women, brought up and educated as we have been, eating and drinking the same food and drink as we do, dressing as we do, experiencing the same pleasures and anxieties as we do. They are human beings living under conditions we are all experiencing today. All of them in their individual ways and in accord with their individual personalities exemplify the basic qualities of saints as I have earlier delineated those qualities. Some of them, such as Mother Teresa and Dorothy Day, pursued their dedication among the lowliest and most abject humans with a love and devotion that we can all admire but alas can seldom emulate. Pope John was one who performed his ministry in the full glare of international publicity and media attention. Thomas Merton exerted his influence from behind a monastery wall with his books and articles, while John LaFarge in his humble, gentle way had an enormous impact on all he met. A Teilhard de Chardin operated on a high intellectual plane with a vision not thoroughly understood even today after hundreds of books and articles have been written about it, while an obscure nun, Edith Stein, gave her life for her faith in one of the darkest eras of human history. And finally Padre Pio, a throwback to the saints of yesteryear as we knew them, made his appeal on a simpler but no less powerful level.

As the saints of yore, they came from all levels of society, some from peasant stock, some from the aristocracy, and still others from middle class families. Some, such as Padre Pio with his reputed miracles, gift of bilocation, and long hours in the confessional; Mother Teresa, lavishing her love on the rejects of the world; and Edith Stein, a martyr, are in the mold we associate with traditional concepts of sainthood. Others, such as

Teilhard de Chardin and Thomas Merton, with their involvement in unpopular causes and theories and resentment of the hand of authority, might give one pause when it is suggested they might be of saintly calibre. And what about a Pope John in one of the most publicized positions in the world. And a Dorothy Day, tirelessly aiding the sick and the weary—a traditional model of a saint—and still a leader in an unpopular cause. And finally a John LaFarge—quiet, humble, unassuming—but oh, so wise, and a fierce battler for great principles.

Yes, they are diverse in what they did and how they did it. But they did have much in common. Each of them would have laughed at the thought that they might be considered a saint. And yet each in his or her own way exhibited those traits that have caused men and women in the past to be venerated as saints. All in their own ways gave their lives to God and the service of their fellow men. There are others living among us as well as these eight who might just as well be singled out as examples of sainthood in our times. To them as well this book gives testimony. They are all vivid and dramatic evidence that the days of the saints are far from over. Truly saints are now—and forever.

John J. Delaney

# DOROTHY DAY

*William D. Miller*

One of the things that has irritated Dorothy Day in these latter days of her life has been the frequency with which people have referred to her as a saint. "That's the way people try to dismiss you," she told an interviewer in 1977. "If you're a saint, then you must be impractical and utopian, and nobody has to pay any attention to you. That kind of talk makes me sick." She did not want to be separated from the world and she had the feeling that many who used the term had that in mind.

However quickly she dismisses those who would canonize her, the fact remains that the overriding passion in her life after she became a Catholic was the pursuit of sanctity. She never wavered in her conviction that this was the true human end and that all the suffering and struggle encountered in the reach for it were passing shadows in the light of its imperishable splendor. "I want to be a saint," she noted in 1952, even though "I know I can only be a little one." She had come to the conviction that this was the only way that she could save herself and the Creation with which she was inseparably bound. "I see around me sin, suffering and unutterable destitution. There is misery, materialism, degradation, ugliness on every side. All I see some days is sin. The problem is gigantic. Throughout the world there is homelessness, famine, fear and war and the threat of war. We live in a time of gigantic evil. It is hopeless to think of combatting it by any other means than that of sanctity. To think of overcoming such evil by material means, by alleviations, by changes in the social order only—all this is utterly hopeless."

This kind of sanctity, bound to the condition of the world, is what Simone Weil, the French-Jewish mystic, begged for in 1943, shortly before her death. The world, she said, needed such sanctity "as a plague-stricken town needs doctors," for "affliction," as she called it, was descending upon humankind with such weight that for increasing numbers all light and hope was being crushed from life. "Affliction is anonymous before all things; it deprives its victims of their personality and makes them into things. It is indifferent; and it is the coldness of this indifference—a metallic coldness—that freezes all those it touches right to the depths of their souls. . . . They will never believe any more that they are anyone."

This sense of the sad desolation into which the world is descending was shared by one of the extraordinarily prescient minds of the twentieth century, Nicolas Berdyaev, the Russian philosopher who lived in exile in Paris and died there in 1948. He saw this time of chaos and suffering as prefiguring the "end of the world," an event that will be characterized by a "transition from a historical Christianity . . . to eschatological Christianity." Traditional, historical Christianity had "grown cold and intolerably prosaic: its activity consists mainly in adapting itself to the commonplace, to the bourgeois patterns and habits of life." But Christ had come to set a heavenly fire on earth. "That fire will not be kindled until the fire of man is set ablaze," when "every moral act of love, of mercy and of sacrifice brings to pass the end of the world where hatred, cruelty and selfishness reign supreme."

While both Miss Weil and Berdyaev, like Dorothy, held the view of a world falling into tribulation, both have likewise emphasized ideas that have a particular aptness to the life of Dorothy Day. Such was the character of her life in her young adult years that one is inclined to believe that she, like so many others in the world today, was all but destroyed by Simone Weil's "affliction." She was confused and lost to the point that she could no longer believe that she was anyone. But even in her depths she clung to hope, and miraculously, she changed. Ignited with the "heavenly fire of Christ," she believed in spite of every doom-auguring sign to the contrary, that the world could be made new —not through the action of governments and programs but by taking love to the very heart of affliction. She believed with Berdyaev that "every moral act of love, of mercy, of sacrifice brings to pass the end of the world where hatred, and selfishness reign supreme." The significance of Dorothy Day to contemporary Christianity is that she overcame the affliction so peculiar to our time to become a revolutionary of the Second Coming.

She was born on November 8, 1897, at Bath Beach, Brooklyn, the third of five children. Her mother, Grace Satterlee, was a person of character and fortitude who came from an area near Poughkeepsie, New York. As a young woman, Grace went to a business school in New York City and there she met her husband-to-be, John I. Day, from Cleveland, Tennessee.

In her autobiographical works Dorothy mentions her mother as a warm and steadfast presence in the home, but of her father she says little—only that he was a journalist and because he worked at night the children saw little of him. But there was more to it than that. John Day was something of an eccentric, gruff and set in his ways. He spent a lot of time at the race tracks, since he covered the racing news, and, presumably be-

cause he became an authority on horses, he was called
"Judge Day." He took a rigid and formal view of
things—even of his children, toward whom he assumed
a kind of Victorian standoffishness. Although he carried
a Bible on his person throughout his life, he would
have nothing to do with religion, even affecting toward
it a strident criticism in the manner of the village atheist. One suspects that as a young man he was offended
by what he took to be the hypocritical piety of some of
his Southern relatives. He was a person who wounded
easily and in whom certain wounds never seemed to
heal. He kept his life manageable behind his formal-
isms, his gruffness, and alcohol, the odor of which
was usually on his breath. There were two things in his
life that brought him comfort. One was his wife. Grace
stood between him and the world—between him and his
children. She was his refuge. The other was the race
track. The sight of a running horse was balm to his
soul.

Dorothy was like her father. She looked like him; she
had his quick intelligence and his interest in books and
writing. There was in her, too, a strain of sensitivity
that made her vulnerable to the insensitivity of others,
and, like her father, she found it difficult to get over a
hurt. Needless to say, John Day never took an understanding view of any part of his daughter's life, and
one is inclined to suspect that some of her extrava-
gances in her younger years were for his benefit. Late
in her life, though, she came to understand him.

When Dorothy was six the family moved to Oak-
land, California, where John Day had gotten a job
reporting race track news. Two years later, in April,
1906, the great San Francisco earthquake cast them all
into the street. John Day got his fine old furniture out
of the battered house—furniture that had been brought
from around the Horn—and sold it on the spot. As soon
as the Days could get out, they left for Chicago. There,

Grace looked the city over for a place they could afford and finally found a row flat on Thirty-seventh Street and Cottage Grove Avenue. It was over a saloon, and Dorothy later remembered the sounds and even the smell from the bar below that came through the floor of her bedroom. It was over a year before her father got a job as the racing editor of the Chicago *Inter-Ocean*. When he did, they moved, and moved several more times, until they found a place they liked. It was a house on Webster Avenue, adjacent to Lincoln Park and the shore of Lake Michigan.

Dorothy recalls with warm feelings this period of her life. Since her friends were not encouraged to visit because of her father's daytime sleeping regimen, she was thrown on her own resources, which is probably the way she preferred it anyway. Her life was school, helping her mother, and reading. She was, and always would be, a devourer of books. Reading was more important to her than sleeping. By the time she was fourteen, she was limiting her sleep to four to six hours at night so she could read. On winter evenings, after the others had gone to bed, she would sit by the coal fire studying her Latin and Greek. When that was done, she would luxuriate in front of the faintly sputtering embers, munch an apple, and read. She observed once that her father supervised her reading so that she would read no trash. He must have had a light duty on this score. She began at the age of six, reading Martha Finley's "Elsie Dinsmore" series, wherein the saintly child Elsie overcomes all manner of tribulations and wins the love of her father. At fifteen she was reading Dostoevsky, a writer whose ideas she would ponder for the rest of her days.

Dorothy, sixteen years old, graduated from Chicago's Robert Waller High School in June 1914. There was no final registration of social accomplishments, but this tall and almost skinny girl, who doubtless was thought of as "different" by her classmates, was recognized for having won one of the three scholarships for college provided by the Hearst Press for Waller's graduating seniors. In August, World War I began, but this colossal tragedy, a sign of the ending of a time, was scarcely noticed by Miss Dorothy Day, who was too consumed with excitement over the prospect of going to college.

She attended the University of Illinois for two years. Although her grade average was high, she was generally an indifferent student. During her first six months she was desperately homesick. She lived alone, did housework and baby-sitting for professors to supplement her meager income, and practically starved herself to buy books. Lonely, she spent her nights reading and then, likely as not, would sleep through her next morning's classes. The experience hurt her and she erected a defense against more laceration by taking on traits that were meant to register upon others her indifference as to what they thought of her. She began to smoke; she affected a crudeness of speech and uttered unladylike words like "damn" and "hell." Registering herself as a Christian Scientist for the University records (her mother had begun to follow this persuasion), she soon proclaimed herself an atheist and joined the socialist club.

In the spring of her first year, though, the harshness of her life was replaced by the radiance of warm friendship. She had written a story about the days of hunger she had known as a student at the University and had submitted it to the "Scribblers," a campus literary group. One of the Scribblers, Samson Raphaelson (later to become a well-known movie script writer), suggested a meeting. One evening he met with Dorothy at a campus coffee shop and brought his fiancée with him. Rayna Simons, from a wealthy Chicago family, was a slight Jewish girl with flaming red-gold hair. Such was Rayna's own temperament that she sensed an intensity and a spirit of quest in Dorothy, and she responded warmly and generously to her. Following that evening Dorothy became a Scribbler, but more than that she began a friendship that, excepting her lifetime closeness to her sister, Della, would be the warmest that she would ever know. As for Rayna, she was, beneath her lighthearted serenity, herself a seeker. Twelve years later she would die of encephalitis in Moscow, just as she was about to enter the Lenin Institute to be trained for a life as a revolutionary. It was only a few weeks after Rayna died that Dorothy became a Catholic.

In 1915, the *Inter-Ocean* failed and John Day again was jobless. Within months, though, he got a job as sports editor with the New York *Morning Telegraph*, and in the summer of 1916 the family moved again. Deciding that she had had enough of college, Dorothy went to New York with the family. The time had come for her to begin her own life, and where else but to New York should a young ambition-filled person go? The trouble was that she wanted to be a journalist, and father John, who had strong convictions as to what a lady should do and not do, said he would have no daughter living in his house who followed a questionable occupation. Dorothy, as hardheaded, kept to her plan and in time she was able to wheedle a job from the editor of the socialist newspaper, the *Call*, located in lower Manhattan on Park Row. Aglow with independence, Dorothy plunged into the Jewish East Side to find a room. Thereafter, she would always claim that her primary citizenship was with this Jewish community.

She worked for the *Call* for eight months, reporting and learning how to put together a newspaper, an accomplishment she would later employ in getting out the *Catholic Worker*. After a time, she came to feel at home in the East Side and in Greenwich Village, making friends of radical journalists and unconventional Village types. One of the former, a *Call* editor, was a young Jew, who, born Irving Granich, later changed his name to Mike Gold. In the twenties and thirties Gold would become the country's leading communist journalist. He and Dorothy were companions, and Dorothy once said that there had been some talk between them of an engagement. In his view, it was Dorothy's sometimes mystical lapses that posed the insurmountable impediment to marriage.

Dorothy was in Washington on April 6, 1917, the day the United States declared war against Germany. She was on assignment, touring with a group of Columbia University student pacifists. The next day she returned to New York to write her story and then, a night or two following, she went to the Anarchist Ball at Webster Hall in the Village. On the dance floor she was espied by a self-styled anarchist whom she knew slightly. Catching Dorothy's attention, the man rushed across the dance floor to embrace her. Repelled by the extravagance of his ardor and the presumption of familiarity it bespoke, Dorothy reacted according to her instinct. She slapped the man, and he, equally startled, slapped her. Thereupon several bourgeois gallants roughly took him out of the hall. Mike Gold's criticism of her for having slapped a fellow radical led her, in a fit of pique, to quit the *Call*.

One day at noon several weeks later as she was hurrying in her long-striding way along Fourteenth Street, she met one of the writers of the radical magazine, the *Masses*, as he was exiting from a saloon. He invited Dorothy to reenter with him but she, in no mood for noontime drinking, would be on her way. So the mellow young man, wishing to oblige, suggested that they go to a German restaurant where Floyd Dell was dining and there they would share his board. This was acceptable to Dorothy, since Dell was already well

known around the Village as one of the most promising
of its writers. At the time, he was acting for Max Eastman as managing editor of the *Masses* and Dorothy, no
doubt, thought she might, with luck, talk herself into a
job. In this she was successful, mainly because Dell,
like Eastman, wanted to get away from the office for a
while. So through the summer of 1917, until it was
suppressed by the government in November, Dorothy
got out the magazine.

That summer Rayna came to visit her and there
were evenings of staying out all night, of sitting on
East River piers and singing revolutionary songs as the
sound of the washing of ship propellers and the whistle
of tugs drifted to them on the cool salt-laden breeze
from the sea. For they were all revolutionaries—
Dorothy, Mike, and the *Masses* artists. The Russian
Revolution, they felt, had just provided the world with
a glorious sign of things to come; beyond Europe's dark
night of suffering lay a spangled new day that would
never end. Did Dorothy believe this? She believed in
brotherhood, in justice, and in raising the human level
of all, but, despite the talk of later years, she was never
a convinced communist. There was something else she
thought: of transcendence, of beauty, and of a community completed that time could never ravage. As she
lay on her back on the pier and looked into the depths
of the firmament whence came the light of an all but
invisible star, this feeling was strong within her.

By November, the work of putting out the *Masses*
had ended and Dorothy was unemployed. It was the
day after her twentieth birthday that she and Mike
Gold were having coffee in a Village restaurant when a
friend approached. It was Peggy Baird, Village artist
and otherwise free spirit. Would Dorothy go with her
to Washington for the next day's scheduled picketing of
the White House in the cause of women's suffrage?
Dorothy had few feminist promptings and did not

know what good it would do the world if women could
vote, but she would go, mainly because it was something to do. Despite her lack of zeal for the cause, she
became a heroine in the eyes of suffragists. When in
the course of picketing she was arrested, she resisted by
biting the hand that was laid upon her to guide her
to her cell. The trouble was that the hand she bit
belonged to the prison superintendent who, in addition
to suffering this injury, had his shins violently kicked.
For this, Dorothy spent six days in solitary confine-
ment. They were days of real suffering for her and
plunged her into a searching examination of her life
and the course it had taken.

She returned to the Village and spent three months
of that frigid winter of 1918 as Eugene O'Neill's bar-
room companion. At least, a legend credits her with
this—a legend she has criticized as being dispropor-
tionate to the facts. Still, she did spend many evenings
with him in the back room of Jimmy Wallace's "The
Golden Swan," on the corner of Sixth Avenue and
Fourth Street. In the dawning hours she would walk
with him through the bitter cold to his room to see that
he was warmly covered, and then she would go to St.
Joseph's Catholic Church on Sixth Avenue and sit for a
while in a back pew. Why? Because it was warm,
she said, and because something there comforted her.
There was little in the way of the romantic that
brought Dorothy and O'Neill together, only that she
was fascinated with the black pall he had cast over his
spirit and that it stirred her to hear him recite Francis
Thompson's *The Hound of Heaven*, which he would do
with alcoholic sonority.

The Village interlude ended tragically on January
22, 1918, when one of O'Neill's friends committed suicide by taking an overdose of heroin at the height of a
Village party. All the merrymakers, including O'Neill,

fled in horror—except Dorothy who alone remained and
held the young man in her arms as he died.

Trying to find herself, she signed up as a nurse
trainee in a Brooklyn hospital. There she stayed for
nearly a year before giving it up because, as she says,
she wanted to write. More to the point, she was desperately in love. Some spirit of ruthless seeking in her nature could lead her to heaven or hell, and in this instance she seemed headed for the latter. The man, a
journalist, had an unstable character and, in his own
way, was ruthless too. It was an impossible affair and
tragedy was its consequence. When she was abandoned, the metallic coldness of Simone Weil's "affliction" took over her soul. She wondered if she could
ever again believe that she was anyone.

In mid-1919, while in this state of desolation,
Dorothy married. The facts of Dorothy's life during
this period were so painful and personal for her that
she has literally excised them from the record, and it is
difficult to re-create them. The person she married was
something of an "idea man" for liberal and radical
publishers, and some of his ideas, it seems, were good.
But his regard for scruples was not high, and, as one
who knew him commented, he seemed to regard marriage as a vehicle for comic buffoonery. He was often
married and as frequently the marriage was dissolved,
either by divorce or some technical invalidation that
he had contrived from the beginning. In any case,
Dorothy was married, and in 1920 she went with her
husband to Europe where she lived, whether with him
or separately, for nearly a year. Then she left and went
to Chicago. She went there, unquestionably, because
the man with whom she had been so desperately and
unhappily in love was working there as a journalist.
She went there thinking, surely, that she could bring
order out of chaos, erase all of the ugly stains of the
past, and even through the strength that she never

doubted she had bring this man to a kind of redemption. It did not work at all. Still, she stayed in Chicago
for two years and, for the most part, her life was as
disordered as it had ever been, moving, as she did,
from one room to another and from job to job. If her
response to the first rupture of her affair had been a
rebound marriage, her response to its final and complete demise in Chicago was to take up again the radical ideal she had held with Mike Gold and some of the
*Masses* journalists in 1917—the Communist revolution
that she believed would bring justice and fraternity
throughout the world. For a while she worked for
Communist leader Robert Minor and did at least one
book review for the *New Masses*. But her activism as a
radical did not quiet her spirit. The only stable and
truly comforting element in her life in Chicago in 1923
was the presence of her sister, Della, who had come to
live with her.

In January 1924, Dorothy and Della went to New
Orleans, where for several months Dorothy did reporting for the New Orleans *Item*. She was in the city
when her book *The Eleventh Virgin* was published, the
text of which she had written in Europe. At the same
time her publishers informed her by telephone that
movie rights had been sold and that her share, immediately available, was $2,500. The book, published by
two Village acquaintances of hers, Albert and Charles
Boni, was an autobiographical novel that carried her
life from its beginning through the bitter collapse of
her stormy love affair.

Why did she write it? Because she was confused,
without a direction, and yet determined, whatever the
cost to herself and others, to do something that would
bring her recognition. It would be an example of the
novel of "realism," more "real" than most. Sometime
later, after she had become a Catholic, the book be-

came anathema to her, which even to mention would cause her face to pale and harden.

Now rich, as she thought, she returned to New York. At the suggestion of her friend Peggy Baird, now Mrs. Malcolm Cowley, she bought a fisherman's shack on the western end of Staten Island. Shortly after this, in the later summer of 1924, she began to live with Forster Batterham. She had met him through a friend, Lily, who was Forster's sister and the wife of rhetorician Kenneth Burke. At the time Forster was moodily languishing in the aftereffects of the Spanish flu. A complete rebel where the manners and customs of conventional society were concerned, he wanted only to be "free," which meant living with Dorothy and fishing in Raritan Bay.

In July 1925, Dorothy realized that she was pregnant, a state that she had begun to believe she could not achieve. She had suffered much, but now her quiet and regulated life on the beach and the knowledge that she would bear a child brought her to a state of near ecstasy. She began to believe again in God, and in gratitude resolved to have her child baptized. Tamar Therese was born on March 3, 1926. It was on an afternoon some weeks later, as Dorothy was wheeling her baby down Hylan Boulevard, that she encountered a nun, a Sister of Charity, from the nearby St. Joseph's Home. However much as a beachcomber and bohemian Sister Aloysis probably viewed Dorothy, the nun nevertheless went about the business of arranging for the baptism in a matter-of-fact way, and in July the rite was performed.

In the time that preparations were being made for Tamar's baptism, Dorothy decided that when she could, she, too, would enter the Church. But what about Forster? In entering into his domestic arrangement with Dorothy he had not reckoned on her getting pregnant, much less becoming preoccupied with religion. Religion was a subject so utterly incomprehensible to him that it was beyond any discussion, and as he observed Dorothy being drawn to it, he must have felt that he was a pointless adjunct to her life. Increasingly he absented himself from the cottage, and when he did return the moments of his presence were filled with such tension that Dorothy became physically ill. Having put off her baptism at the advice of a priest, she waited a year and then decided to end the ambivalence in her situation. One gray day in December, 1927, she went to the Catholic Church at Tottenville and was baptized. This meant no more of Forster in her life—or of any other man, as it turned out.

Dorothy turned to God because she wanted to love. As to the registration of a sign of her new life, it never entered her head to become anything but Catholic. It was, as she said, "the church of the masses," the church of antiquity. "I had reached the point where I wanted to obey," she later wrote. "I was like the child in the *New Yorker* cartoon . . . who said, 'Do I have to do what I want to do today?' I was tired of following the devices and desires of my own heart, of doing what I wanted to do, what my desires told me to do, which always seemed to lead me astray." The Church would provide her with "an instruction and a way of life." Recognizing that her new state would require study and a submission to spiritual direction, she wanted this direction to take her out of chaos, for as it seemed to her, chaos partook of the nature of hell.

In December 1932, Dorothy was thirty-five years old and had been a Catholic for five years. The five years had been a time of desperate struggle just to provide the barest necessities for herself and Tamar, but she succeeded and succeeded alone. It had also been a time of reading, of seeking and taking spiritual instruction, and of living the sacramental life. Yet she felt that she was not doing all that she ought to be doing. She could see that the Church, contrary to the nature of its mission, had been removed from the vital workings of history's process. The world was running wild; the allegiance of men was being claimed by new faiths that asked for sacrifice and even death from those who professed them, but from those who professed the Church there seemed to be no response except to accept things as they were. Middle class propriety, too many assumed, was of itself qualification enough for Church affiliation.

In December, when she went to the communist-organized "hunger march" in Washington, her sense of being outside those forces vying to shape society intensified. The Communists had organized the hunger march; the Nazis could organize the world, but Christianity and the gospel spirit must stand aside. Anguished, she went to the Shrine of the Immaculate Conception to pray for an answer to her feeling of uselessness. "And when I returned to New York I found Peter Maurin—Peter, the French peasant, whose spirit and ideas will dominate . . . the rest of my life."

Dorothy Day has called Peter Maurin a saint and a genius, but this was anything but her feeling when she saw him waiting for her in her flat. He was a short, somewhat stocky man in his early fifties who spoke with a French accent. Speak to her he did, as he had been speaking to all who would listen—professors, businessmen, editors—and when they turned away in weariness, he talked to those clay-faced men who sat on benches in Union Square. Peter, as everyone called him, had talked to George Shuster, editor of *Commonweal* magazine, and Shuster, recognizing that Peter had an idea, sent him to Dorothy Day.

If Dorothy found his incessant talking wearing that first meeting and wished that he would go away, she came in time to appreciate the great sweep of his mind and the utter selflessness that led her to designate him

a genius and saint. This French peasant was no street-
corner haranguer. His intellectual synthesis, the prod-
uct of years of reading and thinking, was so revolutionary that in the contemporary academic world he
would be considered a mad man. He believed that
there was no objective "truth" to which, when discovered, the person should conform. Nor was he looking
for some faulty part in the machinery of the social process which, when diagnosed and corrected, would presumably make all well again. The contemporary problem was not one that came from a pathology of the
social process but one that stemmed from a loss in the
meaning of existence and, with that loss, a breakdown
in the sense of community. The first question was not,
what reform shall we effect next, but, what does it
mean to be human. And as Peter the historian saw it,
there was no more exalted answer to this question than
the level to which the person had been raised by the
Hebrew prophets and by Christ.

It was the Church that Peter saw as the logical and
therefore necessary instrument of re-creation. It was
logical because it brought into history the human ideal
as found in the Judeo-Christian tradition. It was logical
because without that ideal, history had been cluttered,
and never more than in the twentieth century, with the
wreckage of lives victimized by forces that would place
human destiny within the process of time and not in
eternity. It had to be in the Church, thought Peter, because in the objective world of time there was neither
criterion nor source of truth. The Church was necessary
to provide a vision and an instruction. Yes, he would
agree, the Church itself—that part of it that worked in
time—had in some ways ceased to lead. But now, he
said, a critical moment was at hand and the "dyna-
mite" of the Church, as he quaintly put it, must be set
off.

The "idea" that this "gentle personalist," as Dorothy

called him, gave to her was that she, Dorothy, could begin the revolution that would end the world. It would be the revolution that did not end in some supposedly beatified state of time but would end in eternity, where nothing of the "I" would remain—only the "we" of community, complete and final.

What should she do? Begin, Maurin said. Because she was a journalist, she should put out a paper. In the meantime, feed the poor. It all began on May 1, 1933, when Dorothy and a few friends went into Union Square to distribute the first issue of the *Catholic Worker*. The world was seething that day. In Berlin there was a continuous succession of marching and singing groups; in Russia Stalin reviewed a gigantic military parade; and in Union Square fifty thousand assembled to demand jobs and food. In the midst of this melee, Dorothy and several helpers sold their paper for a penny a copy. It was the one paper then, and over the years to come, that called for the great revolution.

Almost immediately the work of putting together a paper took on the character of a movement. "People read about our way of thinking and our way of life and want to join us. They come to visit and remain. Things just happen. Jesus said if your neighbor is hungry, or if your enemy is hungry, feed him. So we took to feeding those who came. . . . The same with sheltering people."

Things just happened, and so happened the Worker houses of hospitality, places where the poor were fed and sheltered. Peter had said to Dorothy that she should begin where she was and with what she had. The world needed hospitality—it needed examples of giving and not taking; it needed signs of communal reconstruction, and where was there a more present and ready task for Dorothy and her young friends who helped her get out the paper than to begin to build community for those dazed men and women who slept

in doorways and lived out of trash cans? The house of
hospitality would be a place where the old world of as-
sertiveness, aggression, and conflict would give way to
community.

The first house of hospitality was Dorothy's flat at
436 East Fifteenth Street. One day Peter brought two
men there to eat. Shortly there were more. In March
1935, Dorothy and her friends moved to 144 Charles
Street, but so great was the pressure for more room
that in April 1936 they moved to 115 Mott Street. The
house, actually two structures—front and rear—was a
donation. Altogether, there were thirty-six rooms available to young Workers and the homeless who were
their guests.

The Workers were housed at Mott Street for fifteen
years, and the style of their life there became that of
succeeding Worker houses. There was little ordered
regularity to things, no scheduled scrubbings and
paintings, and no aseptic odors overriding the smell of
bodies, long unwashed. In the Worker house toilets
ran, overflowed, and faucets dripped. Sometimes rats
ran across the kitchen floor and infestations of vermin
were not unknown.

But young people came to scrub, scrape, and paint.
There was veteran Stanley Vishnewski, the boy from
Brooklyn who crossed the Bridge in 1933 to help
Dorothy get out the paper. There were Eddie Priest,
Charles O'Rourke, and Joe Zarella. Julia Porcelli, just
graduated from high school, had read the *Catholic
Worker* and decided to help. In later years she recalled
her days at Mott Street. Sometimes, she said, people
who read the paper would come down to Mott Street
to visit and were almost invariably shocked when they
found out how poor the Workers were. "Every day
without fail we had very thin soup, and I always remember people remarking on the food. . . . I was always hungry and whenever I got a little sad-looking

Dorothy always said somebody should take me out and buy me a steak . . . that was the best thing, to get treated for dinner." When the visitors saw how poor everyone was, how "we wore the clothes people sent in and we didn't have salaries," they "thought we were holy."

And thus the movement grew, so that by the time of World War II there were forty or more houses of hospitality around the country and six communal farms, all supported by donations from people who read the *Catholic Worker*. These were the bright new days of the movement, when young enthusiasts thought they were igniting a fire that would, even in the time of their youth, light up the world—when young Workers at Mott Street would follow Peter, as he made off for Columbus Circle chanting "to give and not to take," and they responding with "that's what makes man human."

There was crusading excitement as well as a sense of community among young Workers, but life in a Worker house could be oppressive, too. "We write about these things and they sound wonderful," commented Dorothy in the *Catholic Worker*. "The Kingdom of Heaven sounds wonderful, too, but it must be taken by violence. One gives up his life in order to save it. And 'love in practice is a harsh and dreadful thing compared to love in dreams.' People come to join us in 'our wonderful work.' It all sounds very wonderful, but life itself is a haphazard, untidy, messy affair. Unless we can live simply, unquestioningly and solitarily, one might say, in the midst of a mob, then we cease to be a personalist. The more we live with a babbling crowd, the more we must practice silence."

The "harsh" aspects of life in the Worker house increased with the passing years because the world was becoming more fractionalized and impersonal. The "afflicted" were more numerous, and they bore deeper

lacerations of mind and spirit. To be sure, dedicated
and idealistic people still came to help, but the ideal of
community seemed more difficult to achieve. By the
seventies, as the weight of age began to settle upon
Dorothy, she was increasingly called upon to confront
affliction in its seemingly most hopeless and trying
forms. It was then that she, in Simone Weil's phrase,
was "cast at the foot of the Cross."

What was it that has sustained Dorothy in these latter and most trying years of her life? One may believe it
was the hard-won progress she had made on the course
she had set when she became a Catholic. In 1940, as
the world slipped fast into chaos, she began a series of
religious retreats held for Catholic Workers at the
Worker farm at Easton, Pennsylvania. Given by Fathers John Hugo and Louis Farina of the diocese of
Pittsburgh, the retreats were remarkable for their aus-
terity. Held yearly through the war years, they brought
Dorothy to a new level of spirituality. "It was as
though we were listening to the Gospel for the first
time," she wrote. "We saw all things new. There was a
freshness about everything as though we were in love,
as indeed we were." And such was the sense of community that she and her friends felt that they had been
given a "foretaste of heaven."

What did these retreats mean to her? They had
given her a vision of divine love that, except for the retreats, she would never have glimpsed. "I could never
have endured the suffering involved, could never have
persevered." She saw with a new clarity what Peter
had taught. He had emphasized the worth of the person and had made her see how that worth was involved in the redemption of all creation. "Let us make
a world where it is easier for people to be good," he
would say. It was not, as she had supposed as a child,
a matter of living out one's life and then hoping to "go
to heaven." Making her point, Dorothy would quote St.

Catherine of Siena, "all the way to heaven is heaven." The time was now.

The retreats impressed upon her one final, transcending conviction: that all were called to be saints and that the true revolution would occur when persons again sought to answer that call. "Called to be Saints," she said in a leaflet distributed to Workers at the time. To become a saint, she said, *"Is the Revolution,"* giving the phrase her own emphasis. "Too little has been stressed the idea that *all* are called. Too little emphasis has been placed on the idea of mass conversions. We have sinned against the virtue of hope. . . . Where are our saints to call the masses to God? Personalists first, we must put the question to ourselves. Communitarians, we will find Christ in our brothers."

The retreats changed her. She became, more than ever, the woman of prayer. Her waking hours were spent in meditation and reading Scripture—usually the Psalms. "I need this," she said, "to recognize that my first duty in life is to worship, to praise God for his creation, in order to get my mind straightened out so that I can see things in perspective."

In notes that she made in 1949 she wrote this on love:

St. John of the Cross talks of the involuntary pleasure which comes about when the soul is caressed by God and how it overflows into the senses. Is this an experience of that love? All my prayer, my own sufferings, my reading, my study, would lead me to this conclusion. This is a great and holy force and must be used as the spiritual weapon. Love against hate. Suffering against violence. What is two thousand years in the history of the world? We have scarcely begun to love. We have scarcely begun to know Christ, to see Him in others around us. . . . Love is so beautiful and lust so ugly. And all the

world is busy portraying lust—it is in us all. Self
deceit may make us try to cover it up but just as the
corruption of the flesh is there, the rottenness of
decay, the seed of death—so also is the seed of everlasting life.

Love comes at any age, and the remembrance, the
nostalgia is there. And yet who would go back to the
agonies of youth? No, it is a happy thing, a joyous
thing to think of the love to come, the love of God
which awaits us, the fulfillment where we will know
as we are known, when all our talents, energies,
abilities will be utilized, and developed, when we
will be truly loved.


But the retreats did not etherealize her and put her
into a spiritual orbit above the fray. She had always
been controversial and she continued to be. She had
been a pacifist in World War I because she believed
that it was a capitalist war. She produced dismay and
even some outcry when in World War II she proclaimed her pacifism again. "How can we fulfill the
Gospel precept to be perfect as our Heavenly Father is
perfect; how can we follow the precept to love God
when we kill our fellow men? How can war be compat-
ible with such love?"

She has been accused of being overly "naive" on the
subject of communism. It is a matter that she has not
bothered much to argue. Her answer, though, was simple. She was a Christian, a personalist, and the revolution that began with self and proceeded through love
had nothing to do with that which depended upon
strife and killing to change the structure of things. But
then neither could she endorse the acquisitive process
which, in the name of "freedom," had created great
overlordships of capital, which had reduced the person
to an atom, and which had corrupted the body and
spirit of the world, first by physical pollution and then

by propagandizing the masses that the proper object of life was the attainment of all the "things" that capital produced.

Now, in these latter days of her life, Dorothy lives quietly in her room at the Catholic Worker "Maryhouse" in New York. Her pilgrimage is closing, as she knows, and she spends her time in prayer, in reading, and in enjoying the company of her daughter and grandchildren. She made her last public appearance on the afternoon of August 6, 1976, at Philadelphia, a city then filled with alarms over the outbreak of "Legionnaires' disease," as a speaker at the Catholic Eucharistic Congress. She looked frail, and her clothes, which probably had come from a bin at the Worker house, hung loosely on her. She was supposed to speak on "Women in the Church" but, as she frequently did, she talked on what was uppermost in her mind. She spoke of the love of God and the sacred obligation of Christians to take that love into all of creation. She told again of her own experience of the awakening of that love—how "the material world began to speak in my heart of the love of God." Then she reminded her audience that it was August 6, the anniversary of the day that the atomic bomb was dropped on Hiroshima. The twentieth century had become the century of holocausts, she said. After the first World War there were the Armenians, "all but forgotten now, and the holocaust of the Jews, God's chosen people. When He came to earth as Man, He chose them. And He told us 'all men are brothers,' and that it is His will that all men be saved, Japanese, Jew, Armenian." God "gave us life, and the Eucharist to sustain our life. But we have given the world instruments of death of inconceivable magnitude."

Troubled by the great increase in armaments and violence in the world, she had not changed her program. The revolution was still on and, what was more, she already could see it aflame in the Church. Nothing in these latter days of her life could have heartened her more, or confirmed her more in the rightness of her fifty year struggle, than the example of the Church insisting with increasing emphasis on the correctness of many of the positions that she and Peter had taken. Using another phrase of St. Catherine of Siena, she referred to Pope John Paul II as "our dear sweet Christ on earth."

Feeling as she did, she was saddened by the "crisis in faith" that many seemed to be having. How strange it was, she thought, that "our youth dares to be discouraged, with Christ as its leader, with the Church at its back—with its wealth in writings, the very deeds and virtues of the saints to draw upon." As for the complaint she heard at every hand that there was no "freedom" in the Church, she once remarked, "Well, I say we are an example of the tremendous liberty that there is in the Church, the freedom. But we make a point, as Peter Maurin would say: we make a point and that is . . . the layman should go ahead and quit being dependent. I think that is one of the points of the *Catholic Worker*: that you don't need permission to perform the works of mercy. You don't need permission to form your conscience. . . . I mean we go ahead. That's all."

She was critical of the disposition of those who spoke of the Church as "it" or "they"—forever pointing to its shortcomings and asking why don't "they" do this or that. Peter, she remembered, "never allowed people to say, 'they don't do this in our parish. They don't have a St. Vincent de Paul . . . a Christian Family Movement, a Young Catholic Worker, a library, . . . a study club, a credit union, a cooperative.' All work, he would say, begins with an 'I.'"

Peter Maurin was a teacher, and Dorothy, alive to his vision, saw what it meant to strive for sanctity in

this troubled world. With the passion of her ardent nature, she marched into the world of affliction, daring to
be "a fool for Christ," to begin the building of the new
world that Peter had seen. Her life has been remarkable, not only because she overcame her own affliction,
but because she moved to the heart of the world's woe
to lift its weight. A "fool" she is, and in this world of
growing disorder she has been a believable sign of recreation, a sign of the beginning of a new life for
Christianity—the beginning of time-ending Christianity.

Is Dorothy a saint?

Many say so—those who fear that existence is losing
all value and who see her as a hero in the cause of life
—those who find her free when so many are caught in
the slavery of "things"—those who take courage and
hope from her constancy in faith in God and the
Church when the demon of inconstancy gnaws at every
vital structure that supports life.

There are also those who have known her over the
years, who have lived with her in the close proximity of
a Worker house society, who think of her as a saint.
One is Stanley Vishnewski, who died in the New York
Worker house in 1979 after forty-six years with the
movement. In ninety percent of her make-up, Stanley
said, she had her usual run of human shortcomings and
in a few of these she could outdo most people. But
there was, finally, something about her that was different. It was a feeling of something invincible and
absolute about her. Stanley did not like to use the word
"saint." It suggested a person subject to visions and ec-
stasies, he thought. Nonetheless, Dorothy did have a
vision toward which she had moved over all the years
that he had known her. Even her physical appearance,
he said, had taken on the character of that end toward
which her pilgrimage was bound. If what she was was
false and her vision was a mirage, then, said Stanley,
there is no hope for any of us. But Stanley's hope was

beyond all questioning. He *knew* that Dorothy and her vision were true.

## A POSTSCRIPT

Dorothy still lived when the above portrait of her life was written. She died on the evening of November 29, 1980, at Maryhouse, the Catholic Worker house for women, located in a section of New York scarcely equaled for its misery and degradation. Ill with congestive heart failure, she spent the last two years of her life practically confined to her room, devotedly cared for by the people who ran the House. Her pilgrimage ended on November 29, 1980, just as night began to fall. Her daughter was with her.

We live, it seems, in a time when extraordinary efforts are made to gild certain harsh realities of existence with a coating of synthetic fluff. Old age is not usually a golden time, to be whiled away in a Florida resort with the prospect of death's inevitable arrival postponed by shuffleboard in the sun and regular visits to a physician. Time does have its sun-filled moments, but inexorably it annuls whatever expectations of beatitude are made in its name. In old age the senses fade and suffering becomes daily fare. This suffering—this dying—is the essence of pathos.

One feels acutely the pathos of Dorothy's life in its last years. It was not just the physical diminishment from which she suffered—the pain of breathing—it was her growing sense of desolation, of aloneness. So much of the harmony of the world seemed to her to be turning into cacophony, and she could no longer resist it. But through it all she never faltered. Her final days were neither querulous nor despairing. She possessed at her mortal end the certainty that she had always had, even when, as a young woman, she had known days of desolation. As she herself said on several occasions, whatever her suffering, whatever her desolation, she felt that "the Everlasting Arms" were beneath her. This conviction kept her faithful to her commitments, true to her course.

And how could anyone who ever knew Dorothy Day not say that in some mysterious and grace-filled way her suffering became her. For what else could account for that aura of "difference," of goodness, that set her apart from so many of the rest of us?

# POPE JOHN XXIII

## Gary MacEoin

Little about the career of Angelo Giuseppe Roncalli up to the time he was installed as successor to Saint Peter in the bishopric of Rome indicated that he would challenge the more than five hundred million Christians who acknowledged his primacy to question the course on which the Roman Catholic Church had been set for centuries. The fourth of twelve children of a small farmer, he was sent to the minor seminary of Bergamo to begin a career toward the priesthood in 1892, when he was eleven years old. His studies were interrupted by a year's military service in 1902, after which he completed theology in Rome and was ordained priest in 1904.

His first assignment was as secretary to the bishop of Bergamo, and shortly afterwards he began to teach Church history in the seminary. He had already developed an interest in history, especially Church history, that would continue as a major influence all his life. Although he never considered himself an intellectual, he was a learned man, a diligent scholar with a remarkable ability to cut through detail and isolate the essential, and an openness to opinions and attitudes he did not share. At this time he published the first of many historical studies.

Recalled to military service in 1915, he served as army chaplain until 1918. Two years later he moved to

Rome as a promoter of mission activities, an assignment that caused him to travel extensively in Western Europe. In 1924 he was named professor of patrology at Rome's Lateran University. A year later, having been made a bishop, he went as papal representative to Bulgaria. This was the start of a diplomatic career that kept him in the Balkans and Turkey until 1944. It was a particularly enriching experience. While the Catholics of the various rites in union with Rome were his direct concern, he quickly established warm friendships with Orthodox leaders, his historical studies helping him to recognize the harm still being done by the division that had rent the Church for many centuries. From that time onward, Church reunion became one of his obsessions.

Also important was his work for the victims of war, especially for the Jews suffering persecution at Hitler's hands. The unbelievable sufferings and displacements, the physical and moral destruction of millions of people who were in no way responsible for the war, the impossibility of effectively helping more than a tiny minority, all of this left an indelible imprint. Peace joined ecumenism as a value ever uppermost in Roncalli's life. The evil of war was further stressed in his next assignment, as nuncio to France from 1944 to 1952. When he arrived, Church and state were equally rent by hatreds in the aftermath of the German defeat, the collapse of the Vichy regime, and a universal witch hunt for collaborators.

A successful if not particularly distinguished ecclesiastical career was given its appropriate award in 1953 when Roncalli, aged 72, was made a cardinal and sent as Patriarch to Venice. In the limited circles aware of the event, it was seen as a proper completion of a lifetime of simple and solid service to the Church. Even when Pius XII died in 1958, nobody mentioned Roncalli in the lists of cardinals who might be chosen to succeed him.

Cardinals insist that they have the guidance of the Holy Spirit in casting their votes. Enough is known of the sophisticated political processes that characterize the conclaves in which popes are elected to make one suspect that the Spirit exercises guidance in diverse ways. But when a Roncalli emerges, it does give a boost to one's faith in the continuing presence of the Spirit in the Church, particularly at the moments of greatest need.

John started his pontificate in a low key. He was a pastor, he stressed in word and deed. A pastor looked after his flock with tender, loving care, with compassion and understanding. But people don't expect a pastor to be radical, and it took considerable time before there was any significant realization that radical change was in the making. True that within three months he announced his intention of summoning an ecumenical council, a gathering of the more than two thousand bishops from around the world to assess the health of the Church. But he had done this so casually, even insisting that the thought had simply occurred to him out of the void, that the people who were accustomed to running the Church's affairs and telling bishops what to do, the members of the Roman Curia, did not feel threatened. They were accustomed to manipulating popes. They were confident they could drag out the preparations for the council over more years than remained to the old man.

In addition, as Vatican documents dealing with papal diplomacy during World War II subsequently revealed, the Curia had seriously misinterpreted Roncalli as a person, as well as his work, in Turkey. His reports tended to be significantly different from those of other papal diplomats who followed the rigorous rules and administrative practices sanctioned for centuries by the world's oldest diplomatic service, whereas Roncalli insisted on inserting his own reflections, supported by biblical references, to show how God turned human events to his purposes. They scoffed at what they saw as a lack of professionalism, and they misunderstood the docility with which he accepted policy directives contrary to the positions he had recommended, assuming that he was motivated by bureaucratic careerism or possibly even intellectual inadequacy.

What the curialists did not realize is that Roncalli had taken their measure. This is clear, for example, from an entry in his spiritual diary, *Journal of a Soul*, while he was still in Bulgaria. He was not surprised, he noted, at the many trials caused by his ministry. What struck him as strange was that "these are not caused by the Bulgarians for whom I work, but by the central organs of ecclesiastical administration. This is a form of mortification and humiliation that I did not expect and which hurts me deeply." A later reference to "the superabundant cunning and so-called skill of the diplomat" is similarly a clear expression of his judgment on careerists as contrasted with those "who remain faithful to the teaching and example of the Lord."

The reality, as it emerges both from *Journal of a Soul* and from a study of Roncalli's acts as pope, is that he understood deeply his obligation as one who had freely committed himself to work within the Church structures. When his views were overruled, he gave not only formal or nominal acceptance. He did what he was told and gave no hint of his contrary personal convictions. A passage in the *Journal* sets out his principles, and his life demonstrates how he lived them.

"I feel quite detached from everything, from all thought of advancement or anything else. I know I deserve nothing and I do not feel any impatience. It is true, however, that the difference between my way of seeing situations on the spot and certain ways of judging the same things in Rome, hurts me considerably; it is my only real cross. I want to bear it humbly, with great willingness to please my principal superiors, because this and nothing else is what I desire. I shall always speak the truth, but with mildness, keeping silence about what seems a wrong or injury done to myself, ready to sacrifice myself or be sacrificed. The Lord sees everything and will deal justly with me. Above all, I wish always to render good for evil, and in all things endeavor to prefer the Gospel truth to the wiles of human politics."

One of the things that John as pope understood most clearly about the Curia was that he could not use it to bring about the changes he believed the Church needed. Other popes had made that mistake, starting out to reform the Curia as a preliminary to renewing the Church, only to die before they had made a dent on the Curia. He, on the contrary, sensed inerrantly that in the hierarchy of priorities it was more important to transmit some of his own optimism, some of his faith that updating was possible, to the grass roots, to the great masses of believers and nonbelievers waiting for spiritual leadership in an era of deep confusion and doubt.

The first step, apparently simple but in reality very complicated, was to get across to others his awareness that the Church he had been chosen to govern was far from achieving its full potential. On the face of it, that should be easy. But it must be remembered that popes in modern times didn't go around saying such things. During the twentieth century the Church had given the lie to the secularists who had promised that the age of religion had passed. Under Pius XI and Pius XII it had grown in numbers and influence all over the world. The Code of Canon Law promulgated in 1918 had completed the process of welding it into a highly disciplined and excellently organized institution. Its members, especially those in positions of authority, were in no mood to be told that, as well as they were running, it was not in the right direction.

For John, timing was all important. He had a realistic understanding that if one tried to do everything at once or started with the wrong issue, the result was inevitably failure. As he unfolded his dream, it contained three key elements, to which everything else was subordinated. In the first place was the internal reform of the Church, its adjustment to the needs and realities of the contemporary world. His chosen description was *aggiornamento*, the Italian word that means to bring up to date and which through John has entered the vocabulary of all people. The other two elements were Church reunion and world peace. But on one point John was very clear. Until the Church first reformed itself, it could make no real contribution to the other goals. John thus combined an inspired vision of the Church's potential, of the contribution it can make to building a better world by giving what he once called "the light of a great example," with an acute awareness that the image the Church actually projected to outsiders was destructively negative. Until we changed that image by eliminating the defects in our structure and in our behavior that produced it, all our protestations and exhortations would fall on deaf ears. Triumphalism had to go.

The Church had consequently, in John's vision, to stop thinking of itself as outside and above the human condition, the sole custodian of a wisdom the world needed in order to achieve its objectives. Instead, it should understand that its role is more modest. Characteristically, John first broached the idea casually, seemingly tentatively. But like a carefully tended plant it steadily grew in size and consistency, until it was ready to receive full form and official expression in the Second Vatican Council's Constitution on "The Church in the Modern World."

Of particular pertinence in this document is the recognition that Roman Catholics, along with other Christians, must bear a large measure of responsibility for the present plight of the world. Rather than putting all blame on atheists, as some earlier Church documents tended to do, it acknowledged that "believers themselves sometimes bear some responsibility" for the spread of atheism that often arises in reaction to deficiencies in the "religious, moral, or social life" of believers.

Perhaps even more striking is the insistence that the Church "can be abundantly and variously helped by the world in preparing the ground for the Gospel, a help she obtains from the talents and activity of individuals and from human society as a whole." The Church is thus not only present in the world. "A visible organization and simultaneously a spiritual community, it goes forward on the same road as all mankind and experiences the same earthly lot as does the world."

John had gone to his reward before those words were penned, but the concepts they express stand as a monument to his thinking and to his communications techniques. He had first whispered the essence of his revolutionary thought to one he could trust, Cardinal Domenico Tardini, then his secretary of state, on 20 January 1959, just three months after he had been elected pope. In a discussion of the convulsive changes through which humanity was passing, John asked Tardini whether in those circumstances "the Church should be at the mercy of the tides," or whether on the contrary it should not rather be "the light of a great example."

This kind of approach is characteristic of John. He did not start with abstract concepts but with fundamental human experiences, experiences he had lived with, absorbed, and synthesized. From small instances his mind gradually carried him to magnificent visions. His figure of speech was a simple one, appropriate to the unassuming self-image of the speaker. It was also traditional—the Church as the bark of Peter. But it was, nevertheless, radically challenging. Here was the pope suggesting that the Church he headed was perhaps not on the fixed course that its leaders claimed to be steering, but instead rudderless, "at the mercy of the tides." In other words, the Church was not where it would have to be if it was to fulfill its function, and this at a time when the problems of the world—not, be it noted, those of the Church—were such as to be in special need of its contribution.

It was a seemingly casual remark that Tardini may have soon forgotten. In any case, there is no record that he ever repeated it. But John himself did not forget. Having meditated on it for more than three years, during which he developed some of its implications in one of his great encyclicals, *Mater et Magistra* ("mother and teacher"), he decided the time was ripe and minds sufficiently prepared to put it on record. This he did in a talk to a group of visitors in May 1962, just a few months before the opening of the ecumenical council he had summoned. It was during the conversation with Tardini, he recalled, that the idea of calling a council came to him. In fact, only five days after that conversation he had announced to a group of cardinals that he had decided to summon a council.

John reaffirmed this same concept and vision of what the Church's concerns should be, while stressing how different was the view of some Church leaders, when he inaugurated Vatican Council II on 11 October 1962. "In the daily exercise of our pastoral office," he said, using words that for him were extraordinarily harsh, "we sometimes have to listen—much to our regret—to voices of persons who, though burning with religious zeal, are not endowed with too much sense of discretion or measure. In these modern times they can see nothing but prevarication and ruin. They say that our era, in comparison with past eras, is getting worse; and they behave as though they had learned nothing from history—which is nevertheless the teacher of life—and as though at the time of former councils everything was a full triumph for the Christian idea and life, and for proper religious liberty. We feel we must disagree with these prophets of gloom. In the present order of things, divine providence is leading us to a new order of human relations which, by human effort and even beyond human expectation, are directed toward the fulfillment of God's higher and inscrutable designs; and everything, even human differences, leads to the greater good of the Church."

Not less remarkable than his clear vision of his goals was John's patience in pursuing them. I think this can be understood only within the framework of his total life experience. Italian peasants have a profound sense of history. They see themselves as the survivors of thousands of years of oppression and ravaging by one conqueror after another, always the weaker party in the specific contest but always the survivor after each victorious wave had swept past. John's long years as a diplomat, especially in Bulgaria and Turkey before and during World War II, confirmed his attitudes. At one level he worked to lessen the conflicts between religious groups long separated and antagonistic. At another, he tried to aid the victims of the war. In this, his most powerful weapons were patience and an ability to put himself in the place of another whose values and cultural traditions were radically different.

A still more important element in John's patience was his spiritual balance, his unshakable faith. He said his prayers as one on familiar terms with saints and angels. He never claimed a monopoly of good or bad, of truth or falsehood. He saw everyone he met as made in the image of God, and he respected and loved all on that basis. He envisaged himself as a traveling companion of all with whom he came in contact, able to see even in nonbelievers "the faces of friends, the faces of brothers and sisters." As one of his close friends put it, "time does not count for the 'faithful servant' who, having the sense of the eternal, knows that with the help of the Spirit and the expectation of all Christianity, one may accomplish many things in a short time."

When he reached the pinnacle of power that election to the papacy represents, he brought with him this experience and this spirituality. He knew that many of his most important helpers were totally opposed to the changes he was promoting, that some were actively attempting to undercut him. Yet he consistently refused to use his power to remove or silence them. He was absolutely convinced that truth would prevail over falsehood, that people were open to be convinced by example, that anything imposed by force was self-defeating. In his address at the opening of the council he dwelt on this point.

"The Church has always opposed . . . errors. Frequently she has condemned them with the greatest severity. Nowadays, however, the Spouse of Christ prefers to make use of the medicine of mercy rather than that of severity. She considers that she meets the needs of the present day by demonstrating the validity of her teaching rather than by condemnations. Not, certainly, that there is a lack of fallacious teaching, opinions, and dangerous concepts to be guarded against and dissipated. But these are so obviously in contrast with the right norm of honesty, and have produced such lethal fruits, that by now it would seem that people are of themselves inclined to condemn them, particularly those ways of life that despise God and his law or place excessive confidence in technical progress and a well-being based exclusively on the comforts of life. They are ever more deeply convinced of the paramount dignity of the human person and of his perfections, as well as of the duties implied thereby."

This short extract from one of the key speeches of John's life tells a great deal about the man and his political strategy. It is cast in conventional Church language, the kind one would expect from an elderly man who had come from a devout Italian peasant background and spent his life serving the Holy See. It reaffirms the Church's right to proclaim the truth and condemn falsehood and defends the way the Church did this in concrete historical situations in the past. But then comes the hook. It is well concealed, hardly seems to have a barb. Today's errors are so obvious, so self-defeating, that we don't have to waste our time on them. Humankind is developing a level of sophistication and understanding that will enable it to identify these errors and get back on the right path.

I'm not sure that I would want to defend as scientific fact every element in John's evaluation of the progress that humankind has achieved in our times, particularly in relation to the search for truth and rejection of error. But I am overwhelmed by the accuracy and sensitivity of his pastoral approach when placed in the specific historical context in which he was speaking. This context was twofold. The early 1960s were a period of worldwide euphoria. The affluent capitalist states were creating new relations with the nations emerging in Asia and Africa, and with the poor countries of Latin America. The most concrete expression of the euphoria was the Alliance for Progress through which the United States proposed to raise the entire hemisphere quickly to the levels of material well-being and high employment it itself enjoyed. In that context, one could argue persuasively that the world's decision-makers had

grown more convinced of the overriding dignity of the
human person and of the duties that flowed from that
new understanding. The argument would encounter
more resistance today, but I do not doubt that John
would have crossed that bridge when he came to it.
His concern in 1962 was a very specific one, to
preempt the plans of "the prophets of doom" who
wanted to turn the council into a witch-hunt.

But John's strategy carried farther. He was concerned to prevent a widening of the gap between the
Church and those outside that would result from a new
litany of errors or a solemn denunciation of the directions in which the human race was moving. And he
was equally concerned to prevent a reassertion of the
control of truth and opinion within the Church by
those power structures of the Roman Curia which saw
themselves as endowed by Jesus Christ with such a monopoly. In what is undoubtedly the most universally
remembered of his many homely metaphors, he wanted
fresh air to blow through the Church structures. He
wanted a healthy pluralism of opinion within the
Church itself. While maintaining "faithful and perfect
conformity to the authentic teaching," the council
should seek to have it "studied and expounded through
the methods of research and through the literary forms
of modern thought. The substance of the ancient doctrine of faith is one thing, and the way in which it is
presented is another. And it is the latter that must be
taken into great consideration, with patience if necessary, everything being measured in the forms and pro-
portions of a magisterium that is predominantly pastoral in character."

Here John is taking us, in his casual and patient
way, into pretty deep water. He is, among other things,
bringing face to face, two theories of truth. The conser-
vatives, who through the Holy Office and other curial
structures had long been able to monopolize the formu-

lation of Catholic belief and to control its expression, saw truth as something given once for all and guarded in the treasure house of the Church. Whatever issue might arise, the Church had only to go to this store-house to find the answer. And in the context, the "Church" meant specifically those who held the key to the storehouse, the pope and his designated assistants.

Such an understanding of truth had long ceased to make sense to thinking people. Helped by the life sciences to understand the processes by which one searches for the truth and propagates it, they saw as an integral part of the process the need for many theories and opinions to exist in dialectical tension. It was not a question of challenging the existence of objective truth, but rather of stressing that the human condition—by definition contingent and finite—is incapable of en-compassing the totality of truth. At any given moment the most we can hope for is a partial understanding of a truth, an understanding that will expand as we ac-quire more sophisticated intellectual tools and a better grasp of the reality of the universe.

For the medieval Christian the word *transubstantia-tion* was helpful toward understanding the real pres-ence of Jesus in the Eucharist. It matched contem-porary understanding of the nature of material sub-stances, of bread and wine. A radically different un-derstanding of the nature of matter achieved by scientific advances in the twentieth century made the notion of transubstantiation unhelpful to the believer and a stumbling block to those not of the faith. But it was not until John's insistence on distinguishing the substance of the doctrine from the way in which it has been presented that a Catholic theologian could pub-licly offer an alternative and today more meaningful ex-pression, the concepts of *transfinalization* and *trans-signification*, which indicate that in the Eucharist the bread and wine take on a new purpose and a new meaning for the believer. Naturally, the new terms no more exhaust the mystery than did the earlier one. No human words could do that, since the mystery is by definition beyond the grasp of the created mind. But they help us to live with the mystery, opening an alternative perspective to replace the one closed by the progress of scientific knowledge.

Here, for me, we have the essence of John's contribution to the building up of the Kingdom. He understood that the Church was stagnating because of the suppression of free speech and open discussion, a suppression that involved a progressive imposition of legalisms that inevitably destroy the spirit. He knew, from his many years as a diplomat in Europe, that under the surface the Church was seething with discontent, that major theologians and scripture scholars were silenced, frustrated, disgraced, that in consequence the people were not receiving the guidance and the stimulation they needed to achieve their personal sanctification and their social contribution to building up the body of Christ.

I think it is important to stress the practical consequences of this system of government, the way it negates the dynamism and the potential contribution of the faithful, justifying the evaluation widespread in contemporary society that the Church had become an irrelevancy in the struggle of humanity toward a more perfect future. What it does is to ask the people to have a confidence in the leaders that the leaders do not reciprocate. It asks the people to believe that they lack the ability to form serious judgments on religious and related issues, this in a context in which they know they are often far better equipped than the leaders who present themselves as alone authorized to make such judgments. If people are only trusted to obey without question, they are not being trusted at all.

John did not resolve the problem of the relationships

that should exist between those called to the many ministries by which all Christians help to build up the body of Christ, and neither did the ecumenical council he planned and initiated. But he took the first important step, and the council followed his lead by publicly discussing and inviting public discussion of the issues. The altered stress from a strictly hierarchical organization that left all initiative to clerics responded to the growing awareness of the dignity of each person that John stressed as one of the signs of the times. It also came at the moment when the Church was being forced—especially in Latin America, Africa, and Asia— to adjust to a significant decline in the relative numbers of ordained clerics and to find alternative ways of organizing the Christian community. A concrete and significant result has been the growth of grass-roots Christian communities in all parts of Latin America. They have appeared, providentially, precisely when traditional forms of civil and Church organization were proving ineffective to protect the people from the oppression and the Church from the persecution with which reactionary power holders respond to demands for a just economic and social order.

The concept of human dignity, the dedication to the belief that every person is entitled to live a full and useful life, is a constant in John's thought. It is the message of *Mater et Magistra* which opens with the assertion that Jesus Christ established the Church so that all who enter may "find salvation as well as the fulness of a more excellent life." While the Church's specific function is to sanctify souls, "it is also solicitous for the requirements of people in their daily lives, not merely those relating to food and sustenance, but also to their comfort and advancement."

The fulness of a more excellent life, as John envisaged it, called for health services, education, training in skills, housing, social security, leisure and recreation, and the availability of press, cinema, radio, and television. Mindful of his peasant origins, he insisted that the countryside should be as well provided as the cities with highways, transport and market facilities, medical services, schools, housing, pure drinking water, and "the furnishings and equipment needed in the modern farm house."

John was keenly aware of the brief time allotted to him to get his challenging ideas across to the Church and the world. He was seventy-seven when elected pope. His first task, as he saw it, was to start the process of updating, of reform, within the Church. That, he was correctly convinced, would persuade people of all races and beliefs that this venerable institution had a message for everyone, and that it was truly committed to sharing with all in the task of building a better world. One of the concerns he expressed in *Mater et Magistra* was that, although the good life is now available to most of the people of a few affluent countries, "dire poverty" was still the lot of the majority of humans. And he was totally convinced that this situation would continue as long as the powerful and wealthy nations continued to build up ever more costly and more destructive armaments. He had seen the world on the brink of annihilation during the crisis in October 1962 over Soviet plans to install nuclear missiles in Cuba, and he had played a critical—if at the time undisclosed—part in the negotiations that allowed Khrushchev and John Kennedy to back off without loss of face. With the overwhelmingly favorable response from the outside world to the opening of the Vatican Council, he felt he had reached a point where he could be heard with respect and affection by the world audience for which he believed he had a message. In late 1962 he knew from his doctors that his life projection had to be made in months, no longer in years. As he had during the long preparation for the council, he kept an invisible but firm hand on the eight hundred theologians and other experts who had come from all parts of the world to prepare the agenda and to draft amendments and new documents requested by the council. After the first session ended in December 1962, he immediately got the machinery into top gear to prepare for the following one. With all this, he found time to draft what is his most famous statement, the encyclical *Pacem in Terris* ("peace on earth") issued in April 1963, less than two months before his death.

Peace, John wrote, ardently desired by all, is possible only when we have in the world "an order founded on truth, built according to justice, vivified and integrated by charity, and put into practice in freedom." The entire encyclical is a declaration of human dignity and rights as the necessary basis for world peace. It echoes most of the rights stated fifteen years earlier in the United Nations Declaration of Human Rights, proclaiming the nature of each person, endowed with intelligence and free will, to be the foundation on which universal, inviolable, and inalienable rights are based.

The dignity inherent in each person, John stresses, becomes meaningful only in the existential situation of real societies. Here we have again an approach that is characteristic of John and quite different from the appeal to first principles of earlier papal documents. Rights operate only when they are demanded, and the demand for them arises from growing consciousness collectively experienced by human communities. Once again, in a casual and unchallenging context, John withdraws from what had been one of the basic assumptions of earlier social encyclicals. It had been a constant of their teachings that the social order would change when the powerful recognized their Christian duty and accorded to the powerless what was their due. Not so, says John. Don't wait for others to give you your rights. It is only by asserting them, not individually but collectively as a community, that they become real.

John proceeds to list the signs of the times that characterize this process. Workers first claimed their rights in the social and economic spheres, then made claims on the political level and also demanded access to learning and culture. Women have ceased to tolerate being treated as inanimate objects or instruments, claiming instead in domestic and public life equality of rights and duties. The inhabitants of lands long held as colonies reject controls imposed on them from the outside, especially when racial discrimination is a factor. Most states organize themselves juridically through a written constitution that includes a charter of basic human rights.

All of this gives an insight into the subtlety of John's thinking. Every human being has always been endowed in principle with basic human rights. But it is only when we become conscious of our rights and organize to vindicate them that they have a concrete meaning. And in this process, it is not the Church that historically has taken the lead, even though the principles it affirms should have placed it in the forefront. Instead, it is the world that played the principal part in awakening the Church to the dignity of each person.

The message is twofold. There is a generous acknowledgment of the positive values developed through history by the entire human race in the process of continuing creation. There is a challenge to the Church to spend less time looking inward on itself, to concentrate instead on listening more attentively to what the world has to teach it; to recognize in particular that its members—as men and women of the twentieth century—reasonably and properly demand the same respect for their inalienable rights from the Church as they demand from the state and from society.

Pope John died after an agonizing illness on 3 June 1963. To the very end he worked at an incredible pace, as though everything depended on him, yet with a calmness and detachment that expressed his recognition that the outcome is in the hands of God. "Don't look so worried," he told his physician in a typical expression of his humor, kindness, and serenity. "My bags are packed, and I am ready to go." But while he waited, he was never for a moment idle. As he lay dying, he dictated his last testament, in which he distilled the entire message he had for the Church and for the world. "Now more than ever, certainly more than in past centuries, our intention is to serve people as such and not only Catholics; to defend above all and everywhere the rights of the human person and not only those of the Catholic Church. It is not the Gospel that changes; it is we who begin to understand it better. . . . The moment has arrived when we must recognize the signs of the times, seize the opportunity, and look far abroad."

Here John—on his deathbed—challenges us as Christians to a profound conversion, a collective reorientation that shifts the center of our religious concern from the ecclesiastical institution to our historical consciousness as human beings. By thus proclaiming the end of the ecclesiocentric system, John opened religious history to the invasion of social, political, and racial questions on a universal scale.

Conversion is painful, and we should not be surprised if many within the threatened institutions resisted and continue today to resist. But a truth once enunciated has its own dynamics. John's truth dominated the Vatican Council after his death, and it has since continued to spread throughout the universe of human consciousness. In the 1980s, in a world in which the human rights of the vast majority are trampled upon as never before in human history, we find the Church in solidarity with the poor and oppressed, sharing their martyrdom and also sharing their fatih in the justice of their struggle. Here we have the first fruits of Pope John's unique vision, a vision that is steadily penetrating the course of history and entering into the universal consciousness. To paraphrase one of John's favorite comments, when we have all internalized this vision so that our acts are our witness as Christians, it will no longer be necessary to expound doctrine because there will be no more unbelievers.

John's ultimate accomplishment is that he offered us a radically different understanding of what it means to be a Christian. This he did in a way as profoundly human as it was profoundly spiritual. When on 28 October 1958 the papal electors chose the benign, rotund, constantly beaming, elderly peasant from northern Italy, there were few if any indications that he would make a major impact on the Church, still less on the world. All we had was a harmless old man who would not tamper with the complicated machinery, giving his colleagues a breathing space before choosing a worthy successor to the sublime Pius XII. As John noted in his diary: "When the cardinals of the Holy Roman Church chose me to assume the supreme responsibility of ruling the universal flock of Jesus Christ, everyone was convinced that I would be a provisional and transitional pope."

By the time John died less than five years later, he had become an object of reverence and affection for people of all faiths and of none. But it was far from clear if he had really changed the history of the Church and the world. There was no guarantee that the ecumenical council he had convoked would achieve the objectives he had formulated for it, and indeed there still remains uncertainty as to how successful it was.

He had, however, started processes that gradually came to infuse many Catholics with a new vision of their role. Years earlier, when in Bulgaria, he had noted in his diary that he was planting a few seeds here and there that he was confident would, in God's due time, sprout and produce abundant fruit. His seedlings continue to flourish. We are expanding our Christian commitment beyond the negative formulations of the Code of Canon Law and of theological manuals written by canon lawyers. Our dominant concern is no longer simply to avoid mortal sins and the occasions of sin. We have ceased to see the Church as a fortress attacked on all sides by enemies, a fortress we have to defend by engaging in activities dictated by Church superiors who alone are endowed with the gift of judgment.

Such negative attitudes, understandable in the climate of the Reformation and Counter-Reformation, had become dysfunctional in the pluralist society of the twentieth century. Catholics now mingled with people of all faiths and of none, whose specializations ranged through the physical and life sciences. They were, by definition, the enemies assailing our fortress. Yet their typical way of living, their concerns, and their commitments negated the assumptions that were our first principles. When they criticized the Catholic Church, as many of them did, they criticized aspects that we could not in good conscience defend. When agnostics or theists rejected the notion of a God who inflicted everlasting punishment for a single infraction of eternal laws or scoffed at the idea that eternal happiness was the reward for learning to jump through theological hoops, were they being unreasonable? The less we thought about such issues, the simpler our life as Catholics. But also the more meaningless.

Today, thanks to Pope John, we can face such issues honestly. We can see our faith as less a system of truths than as a way of life. We have been given life and

talents not to spend them on a multiplicity of intrin-
sically meaningless activities, but to help take the
world a little closer to the perfection of which the Creator saw it capable when (in the Genesis myth) He
handed over the continuing creation to the intelligent
beings He had made. We see service to our neighbor as
the most acceptable and meritorious way to worship
God. We understand that the Christian may not be
neutral as between powerful oppressors and powerless
oppressed people, but must imitate Jesus in a prefer-
ential option for the poor. We see the essential Church
as not limited to clerical-dominated institutions but as
waiting to be born in grass-roots communities of peasants and slum dwellers inspired by the Spirit to become the artisans of their own liberation from spiritual
and material deprivation. We owe our allegiances as
determined less by institutional affiliation or creedal
affirmation than by identification with all who share a
commitment for a future based on justice and bonded
with love.

Only a very extraordinary person could accomplish
such miracles. Such indeed was John, a very simple
and yet a very complex person. Even when he knew he
was dying, he remained always smiling and relaxed,
giving an impression of balance, serenity, and goodness
that one associates with those who pray a lot. A softly
contoured face nevertheless revealed enormous energy
and firmness of decision. He sought to pacify rather
than affront, preferring patience to cutting knots, and
always respectful of opposing opinions. When someone
deplored the conflicts that developed in the council
debates, his response was that "we are not friars singing in a choir." He liked to quote a French epigram:
"Some things one must oneself do; some things one
must make others do; and some things are better left
undone." But he would yield only to the extent that
principle allowed. Tenacity was joined to astuteness.

Far from being the Modernist that some detractors labeled him, John was deeply attached to tradition, especially in matters of doctrine. New formulations, yes, never a watering-down of substance. And where doctrine was not at issue, he easily adjusted to contemporary revolutionary changes in sciences, economics, morals, and politics. His words, though easy to understand, reached into the profoundest mysteries of faith.

Intuitive rather than cerebral, he thought in terms of fundamental human experience more than in concepts, and it was his genius to synthesize these experiences into a coherent world view and to project them in ways that made sense to people of diverse backgrounds and cultures. The rhythmic natural influences of his native village were a lifelong influence. Asked by some bishops what he would like to do after the council, he replied without hesitation: "Spend a day tilling the fields with my brothers." He loved his brothers deeply, respecting them as the simple peasants they were. Unlike his predecessors, he refused to give them titles or to change their life-style. In the same way in which he loved his brothers where they were, he loved all peoples where they were. Because of that love, he labored as few popes have done to respond to the prayer of Jesus "that they all may be one." And because of his ability to express his love in word and deed, he succeeded more completely than any of his predecessors in convincing the world of his sincerity. Even those who seldom or never prayed were touched by the man who said his prayers as one who lived with saints and angels. He was a man for all people and for every age because he was faithful to the past, devoted to the present, and open to the future.

# JOHN LaFARGE

*Edward S. Stanton*

Father John LaFarge was not an ordinary prophet. He never seemed to make any noise, just as he never seemed interested in making an impression. He spoke in gentle tones. He wrote with restraint. His eyes were infinitely kind. He was a man of sweet reasonableness. He was cultured, brilliant, and holy.

When he died the Second Vatican Council was just beginning. Had he lived, even to the end of the council, he would have rejoiced that there was a new spirit abroad in the Church and that official documents were calling for a more lively liturgy, a new openness to other religions, and greater concern for the poor and for victims of discrimination. This was the world in which he was at home, even before it was officially accredited. In 1963 he was a prophet whose day had come. The American Church historian, John Tracy Ellis, remarked that Fr. LaFarge was one of the small number of charismatic people who produced the seminal ideas that bore fruit in the flinty soil of the American Church once the sluice gates had been opened by Pope John XXIII and his ecumenical council.

John LaFarge was a gentle man. *Time* magazine once commented that he was born at the same time into the Catholic Church and into the social register. In Newport, R.I., on February 13, 1880, he was born the

youngest of nine children. William and Henry James
had introduced his mother and father to each other.
Having taken instruction from Father Isaac Hecker, his
mother, Margaret Mason Perry LaFarge, entered the
Catholic Church shortly after her marriage. Her beauty
made her the center of attraction for the youth of Newport. She was sensitive, highly intelligent, and heroically patient.

John's father was educated at St. John's College,
which later became Fordham University, and at Mount
St. Mary's College in Emmitsburg, Md. After three
years of study in Paris where he met many of the Pre-
Raphaelites, he rented a studio in Newport and in time
became the leading mural painter in this country. He is
famous also for having revived the lost art of stained
glass portraiture.

Fr. LaFarge came from a rich family heritage. Some
of his forebears were Benjamin Franklin, Commodore
Oliver Hazard Perry of Lake Erie fame in the war of
1812, and Commodore Matthew Galbraith Perry, who
in 1853 opened up Japan to the western world. One
uncle, Thomas Sergeant Perry, was professor of English
at Harvard, and another uncle, Dr. William Pepper,
was provost of the University of Pennsylvania. One of
his cousins, Miss Agnes Irwin, served as dean of
Radcliffe College, and another cousin, Miss Lilla Perry,
was a member of the Cabot family of Boston. Finally,
on his father's side, a grand uncle had served as consul
general for the pope during the days of the Papal
States.

As a child John attended the public schools of Newport and became an eager student. Meanwhile his
mother, and sometimes a visiting relative, would read
to him after supper by the light of an oil lamp. As they
made their way through most of Charles Dickens, Anthony Trollope, and Jane Austen the characters in these
books became part of John's daily life. At the age of

ten he was editing a monthly magazine, *The Sunlight*, which he sold to family and friends for two cents a copy; by the time he was thirteen he had twice read Boswell's *Life of Johnson*.

After he graduated from Rogers High School in Newport the question arose as to where he would go to college. Even though he had already passed the preliminary examinations at Columbia University, Theodore Roosevelt, then police commissioner of New York City and a close friend of John's brother Grant, prevailed on him to attend Harvard and to specialize in the classics. At Harvard, in addition to studying piano and organ for four years, John elected to major in Latin, Greek, Hebrew, Syriac, and Aramaic. This was not strange, for as a child he had already developed considerable familiarity with French, Russian, Polish, Danish, Swedish, Icelandic, and Gaelic. Before he died he had learned twenty-three languages.

He found Harvard challenging—always to his mind and sometimes to his faith. Because of this he regretted that the sermons and services offered in the local Catholic church were inadequate. In fact, the memory of poorly prepared sermons at St. Paul's Church troubled him so much that three years after he finished college he made a trip to Portland, Maine, to visit Bishop William O'Connell who was rumored to become the successor of the aging Archbishop Williams of Boston. John pleaded that Harvard students be provided better spiritual direction, and even recommended that the Jesuits be allowed to assign a chaplain there. O'Connell did come to Boston, better services were provided, but the Jesuits were not sent to Cambridge. However, many ideas which John LaFarge set forth in 1904 about the need of a special chaplaincy for university students were, in some measure, responsible for the formation of Newman clubs across the country.

In late June 1901, at twenty-one years of age, the

young graduate of Harvard College's first class of the
twentieth century decided to prepare himself for the
priesthood. This was not a sudden decision. As he tells
the story in his autobiography, *The Manner Is Ordinary*
(written at the request of his superior when he was
over seventy years of age), the thought of becoming a
priest had been "the all-dominating idea of his life" for
nine or ten years before he graduated from college.
Like all vocations, his call grew somewhat mysteri-
ously. He never served Mass as an altar boy. Very few
of his playmates were Catholics. Newport society was
not conducive to the flowering of a priestly vocation.
Priests of his acquaintance were excellent men, he
knew, but they did not appeal to his imagination. The
first reaction of his admittedly "priggish" mind to the
life of seminarians was that they were "singularly
unkempt." So, there seems to have been no one whose
personal influence encouraged him to pursue the priesthood.

It is true that his mother, whom he loved dearly,
"rather approved of the idea," but John claimed that
"she never pushed it in any way." When John was
seven years old his mother had consecrated him to the
Blessed Virgin at the main altar of St. Mary's Church
in Newport, and for some years thereafter he always
wore blue suits as a token of that consecration.
Throughout his life he felt that he belonged to Mary in
some special way and that, in return for her watching
over him night and day, he owed her an extraordinary
fidelity in thought and action. Moreover, when he was
ten years old and was receiving his first holy communion in the Arch Street Convent of the Religious of the
Sacred Heart in Philadelphia, he wore a white ribbon
which led him to the resolution that his soul should as
far as possible remain white all his life long.

Books more than people were the decisive influence
in determining his vocation. As a small child he read

through the Douay version of the Bible three times and kept it close to his pillow at night. The second important book was a copy of the Latin Missal, given to him by the assistant pastor of the local church. And the third was Cardinal Manning's *The Eternal Priesthood.* As he looked back on the dawning of his vocation he said that the thought of Mass attracted him most of all "and particularly its closeness to our Lord Jesus Christ himself, for whose personality I felt an intense attraction and for whose friendship I increasingly longed."

The seminary John decided to enter was located in Innsbruck, Austria. That was where Father Thomas Gasson, S.J., an Englishman by birth, had taken his theological training a few years before. During John's years at Harvard College Father Gasson was serving as professor of philosophy at Boston College. Once a week for four years John would cross the Charles River and journey into Harrison Avenue in Boston to visit this saintly man for confession and spiritual advice. A strong friendship grew between these two men, and John thought that what was good for Father Gasson would be good for him.

But before he could break away to prepare himself for the priesthood in the diocese of Providence, R.I., there was one more barrier he had to hurdle. John's father had other plans for his son and for this reason he was reluctant to give his approval to the idea of John hiding himself away in a seminary. But Theodore Roosevelt once again came to his support, maintaining that God had sent young John certain graces and that it would be folly not to allow him to follow them. As Fr. LaFarge put it later, "T.R. was an eloquent advocate and his counsel won the day."

As John was boarding ship for Europe in the summer of 1901, his mother begged him, "Don't let them make you a Jesuit." He solemnly replied, "Mother dear, nothing can ever make me a Jesuit." Years later neither Mrs. LaFarge nor John could explain why she had made this remark. John had never considered the idea of becoming a Jesuit, much less had he talked about it. It appears, however, that four years of intellectual and spiritual guidance under the Jesuits at Innsbruck did have its effect. The thought of joining the Society of Jesus seeped into his soul gradually, and by the time he had finished an eight-day retreat during his fourth and final year of theology the thought of God calling him to the religious life flooded his inner being and filled him with peace. When, the following summer, he presented himself to the bishop of Providence to explain that he did not think it was his vocation to become a diocesan priest, Bishop Matthew Harkins was very understanding and allowed him to be ordained without any ties to a diocese.

Later that summer he applied for admission to the Society of Jesus and entered the novitiate at St. Andrew-on-Hudson in the fall of 1905. A circumstance associated with his journey to the novitiate is commemorated in the United States Congressional Record (Dec. 3, 1963). It seems that he was stumbling along under the weight of several bags and was late arriving at Grand Central Station. Thinking the train might depart without him, he shouted, "For Heaven's sake, open the gate and let me through. I must make this train; I'm leaving the world."

He did indeed make it and arrived at Poughkeepsie, N.Y., on November 13, 1905. But his leaving the world and submitting himself to a regimen of prayer and austere living only prepared him to return, with a new vision of God's presence, to the world that he had left a short time before. After Fr. LaFarge died, Fr. Thurston N. Davis, S.J., editor in chief of *America*, who knew him as well as any Jesuit, wrote that recollection and prayerfulness were his most outstanding characteristics:

Fr. LaFarge could turn off distractions and turn on his interior life with God and ideas faster and more effectively than anyone I have ever met. The secret of it, I suppose, was that he lived in both worlds all the time. The City of God and the City of Man were so fused in his high spirit that he could pass from one to the other without having to show his passport.

After two years of formation at St. Andrew-on-Hudson, Fr. LaFarge was asked to teach freshman English, Latin, and Greek at Canisius College in Buffalo. Possibly because, according to his own admission, this teaching assignment was difficult and bewildering he taught there for only one semester. During the second semester he taught the same subjects at Loyola College in Baltimore. There the atmosphere was somewhat more congenial but it appears that he was not a very successful teacher. This may explain why two of his Jesuit provincials told him during his lifetime that they did not know what to do with him.

At any rate, in the fall of 1908 he entered Woodstock College in Maryland to begin further studies in Scripture, canon law, and theology. He had not been there long when his father died. This ordeal drained his energies so seriously that one day the superior of the community, Fr. Anthony Maas, came to his room and proposed that his studies were too much of a strain for him and that he should undertake less demanding work. "You have a choice," he said, "either of being a live jackass or a dead lion. Personally, I think it is better to be a live jackass."

That did it. By moving away from the strain of studies he did preserve his health, but he deserved the title "live jackass" about as much as St. Thomas Aquinas deserved to be called "the dumb ox." Calling off his studies at this point was a heavy blow, for, since the days when he was studying biblical languages as an undergraduate at Harvard, he had entertained a secret dream that one day he might earn a doctorate in Sacred Scripture and teach in a Jesuit house of studies. It is interesting to note that later in life he referred to this decision at Woodstock as one which forced him to give up the idea of pursuing a "strictly intellectual *speculative* career." Henceforth he was to be involved in the practicalities of his pastoral life and he developed an intellectual *pastoral* career.

Leaving Woodstock, he was assigned to serve as chaplain in the hospitals and prisons on Blackwells (now Roosevelt) Island in New York. As he boarded the ferry at the foot of East Seventy-second Street and the East River, he was nervous and apprehensive. That isolated island out there had a bad name; to be sent to Blackwells Island was only short of being sent to Sing Sing. Four separate institutions on the island housed over five thousand patients and prisoners to whom he ministered for eight exhausting months. But this period proved to be a salutory experience—even a turning point—in his life. Counseling and consoling the sick and delinquent opened his eyes to the need of human warmth in the life and manner of a priest. As a boy of sixteen he had once been chided for cultivating only his intellect, while neglecting the affectionate side of his nature. A priest who knew him well had said to him, "What you need is less brains and more heart." Blackwells Island, for all its bleakness and tragedy, was a place where a scholarly young priest learned to love in a new way.

After nine months in New York City he was asked to join five other Jesuits at Leonardtown in St. Mary's County, Md., where the Potomac River enters the waters of Chesapeake Bay. Here the Jesuits had been ministering to Catholic people since they first arrived in the *Ark* and the *Dove* in 1634. Except for his year of "tertianship" (the final year of spiritual formation for all Jesuits) he remained here for fourteen years.

This tour of duty marked a definite turning point in his life. Here he served his apprenticeship and prepared himself to make his most important contribution to the life of the Church in this country.

At Leonardtown he found that at least forty percent of those who lived among the rolling hills of the counties of southern Maryland were blacks. LaFarge made every effort to dig into black history, trying to understand their culture and to drink deeply of their spirit.

The priests at Leonardtown took care of several missions. In the early days the new curate had the use of a twenty-five-year-old horse named Morgan. Morgan had belonged to his predecessor, Fr. Clement Lancaster, who, as Fr. LaFarge quickly learned, was a very sociable man. As they trundled along the country roads Morgan would instinctively pull the buggy through certain gates and up to houses where apparently Fr. Lancaster had been wont to stop and visit. If Morgan met anyone traveling in the opposite direction he would come to a dead stop "expecting a little conversation to be started up." However timid and diffident his new driver might have been before coming to Maryland, Morgan made sure that he had a quick course in public relations.

Along the way to the far-flung mission chapels the priests were accustomed to stay overnight with parishioners. The people expected the priest to know their homes and take an interest in all their affairs. As he made his way from place to place with Morgan and the buggy, and later in a Model T Ford, he prayed constantly, thought out his sermons and catechetical instructions and patiently endured the vagaries of the weather. The roads he traveled were not hard-topped but made of gravel. He often found that at country funerals the words, "Remember, man, that thou art dust and unto dust thou shalt return" applied in the *present* tense.

The assistant country pastor recognized very early that the poor people needed better education. Public schools, with very few exceptions, were one-room affairs, inadequate for the white children and a mere farce, in many cases, for the blacks. Therefore, Father LaFarge obtained permission to go to Washington, Baltimore, and New York City to visit friends in the hope of raising funds. Many cooperated generously. During his thirteen years of priestly ministry in Maryland he was instrumental in opening eight schools which were staffed by religious sisters and brothers and well trained laymen and laywomen. And he contributed to the children's appreciation of one of the glorious traditions of the Church of Rome by teaching them Gregorian chant.

Among the schools he founded the most famous was the Cardinal Gibbons Institute. With the help of $8,000 from Cardinal Gibbons, $35,000 from the Knights of Columbus, and gifts from Mother Katherine Drexel and her sister Mrs. Edward Morrell, he planned and built a trade school for black boys and girls. The school was staffed by Mr. Victor Daniels, who had previously taught at Tuskegee Institute in Alabama, his wife, and a small group of religious sisters. In the board of trustees that was organized to support and direct the school one can see indications of LaFarge's ecumenical spirit; the committee included whites and blacks, Protestants and Catholics, southern Marylanders, Washingtonians, and people from all over the country.

Hundreds of young blacks were thus prepared to earn a good living within this rural community. The doors of the institute were first opened in the fall of 1924 and were closed in 1934. Two factors contributed to their closing: first, the Depression made it difficult to collect the necessary funds; and secondly, the opening of a naval air base nearby meant that jobs more attractive than farming were offered to the local people.

Even though the school closed down after only ten years, the founding father considered that it had opened a door to a new vision of the capacities of the blacks, both in their own eyes and those of the public at large. And, in his judgment, it had worked "as a powerful instrument with which to awaken the dormant consciences of the Catholic public who were forgetful of the abnormal situation of the blacks in the Catholic Church."

During his days in Maryland, Fr. LaFarge wrote several articles about the charm, beauty, and healthiness of life in a rural community. He hoped the farmers would stay on the land because he knew from his experiences at Blackwells Island how easily people from the country could be swallowed up and "contaminated" by life in a big city. For this reason, he became one of the first supporters of Bishop Edwin O'Hara and Monsignor Ligutti in the work of the National Catholic Rural Life Committee.

In the fall of 1926, because of his broad pastoral experience and his writing ability, Fr. LaFarge was invited to join the staff of *America,* the Jesuit weekly journal of opinion. Here he spent the rest of his life writing 764 signed articles and countless "current comments," attending editorial board meetings, entertaining guests, delivering lectures, reviewing books, and correcting galleys. He also wrote nine books.

The residence and editorial offices of the Jesuits on the staff of *America* were located on West 108th Street, near Riverside Drive and not far from Grant's Tomb and Columbia University. It was a quiet, even sedate, area of the city. But the section that interested him

most was Harlem, which was located farther up the island of Manhattan and somewhat to the east.

Through the years he wrote his share of articles on
political, social, liturgical, and cultural affairs but the
concern, above all others, that preoccupied him was
the plight of the blacks. He saw them as the "most
neglected segment of American society" and as the
"weakest link in the Catholic Church." In fact, there
were at that time about thirteen million blacks in this
country, of whom only a quarter of a million were
Catholics. And there was only one black priest in the
entire country in 1931, Fr. Norman Dukette. The
blacks deserved, Fr. LaFarge said, "the best the white
man has to offer." In an early article he even claimed
that the whites should consider the blacks as their
"wards." However, once he began to have dialogues
with the leading members of the Catholic black community in New York City, his attitude changed from a
certain tone of condescension to a sense of real partner-
ship.

It happened this way. He called together a group of
twenty-five men who were prominent in public life or
who showed promise of being able to influence public
opinion. All the members were indeed black. When the
rules for the organization were drawn up, however,
they described the membership as consisting of black
Catholic business and professional men, with "such
other persons as, in exceptional circumstances, the
members shall consider particularly qualified to take
active part."

They discussed racism in American society and what
they could do to counteract it. The first meeting went
so well that they decided to continue meeting every
month. At their meetings Father LaFarge led them in a
"dialogue Mass." While the celebrant spoke in Latin
the members of the congregation recited many of the
prayers and readings in English. This was an antici-

pation of what the Mass would be thirty years later as a result of the reforms of the Second Vatican Council.

After Mass they retired to another room where they studied together the life of Christ and its social implications, especially as they are expounded in letters of Pope Leo XIII and Pope Pius XI.

Soon they organized a retreat. Because New York Church authorities in 1928 were not known to be particularly enthusiastic towards Fr. LaFarge's venture, the group went to Tenafly, N.J. There they continued to meet once a year from Thursday night until Monday morning. For as long as he was able, Fr. LaFarge delivered the conferences to help these men with their prayer.

They came home each time with a new vision of what they could do to secure for their families and friends better housing, jobs, education, and social acceptance. Few, if any, became militant. Their director never advocated militancy; he was eminently noncontentious. But he did see the need of helping these men broaden their horizons so that, in the light of the Gospel, they could better understand and work for freedom.

In Latin America within the last few years many Catholic writers have been developing what is known as "liberation theology." In their view a key step is to bring the poor and the underprivileged together in small groups where, through prayer and study, they can discover how God wants them to become free and aware of their human rights. They call this "the raising of consciousness" or "conscientization." Almost fifty years ago, and before the word was coined, Fr. LaFarge was engaged in conscientization in New York City.

Soon this group, known as the Catholic Laymen's League, was organizing forums once a month in any section of the metropolitan area where they could find

an audience. And through the kindness of Fr. Gillis,
C. S. P., editor of *The Catholic World,* they often spoke
on racial matters over the radio.

On Pentecost Sunday, 1934, they gathered a group
of 800 in New York's Town Hall for an important
meeting. Speakers like Fr. Gillis, Michael Williams of
*Commonweal,* Mr. Elmo Anderson and Mrs. E. P. Rob-
erts of the New York Urban League, spoke strongly
about the neglect and persecution of the blacks by the
"dominant race that achieved and maintained its domi-
nance with injustice, brutality, falsehood and hypoc-
risy."

Shortly after this meeting, with the strong support of
Dorothy Day and others like her, the Catholic Interracial Council was formed. George Hunton, a dedicated
Catholic lawyer, who from 1931 until he died was Fr.
LaFarge's friend, counsellor, and coworker, became the
editor of *The Catholic Interracial Review.* Mr. Hunton
in his autobiography, *All of Which I Saw, Part of
Which I Was,* observed that the members of the council "had minds of their own," that they made their own
decisions and that Fr. LaFarge encouraged this. Thus
he was far ahead of his time, for Catholic Action was
not widely accepted in this country and those who
promoted it thought that the laity should be mobilized
to carry out the directives of the *clergy.* But that was
not Fr. LaFarge's idea. In Mr. Hunton's words, Fr.
LaFarge

> wanted a true lay organization, its officers and direc-
> tors responsible for determining policy and super-
> vising its execution, the role of its chaplain merely
> one of consultation in matters bearing on Catholic
> teaching and practice.

And the hope was that other councils like the one in
New York would be established throughout the coun-

try. Priests would be needed, however, to serve as chaplains. Around this time, therefore, Father LaFarge organized the Northeastern Clergy Conference on Negro Welfare. Among the members were Father Gillis, Father Harold Purcell, C. P., editor of *Sign* magazine, and Father Joseph Corrigan, who later became a bishop and rector of Catholic University. At their meetings which stretched out over ten years, these men dedicated themselves to "organize propaganda for the spiritual welfare of the Negro and its material implications."

After these foundations had been laid the Interracial Council in New York was in a position to sponsor other groups. Before he died Fr. LaFarge saw a string of forty Catholic interracial councils spanning the entire country.

Fr. LaFarge viewed the Church as "the universal body of those who are one in Christ," as the "prophet and spiritual agent of unity," and as the "only entirely consistent champion of human rights in the world today." He felt she should never be closed off from others but should always remain open to a wider community. "Group selfishness," he wrote, "is a principle of corruption."

He revered the Bishop of Rome and looked upon papal statements "not as the arbitrary dicta of venerable religious functionaries" but as carefully thought-out reflections on the social demands of the Gospels. What the popes put forth in traditionally lofty language La-Farge applied in simple terms to the world he knew. The story of the good Samaritan meant for him courageously enduring the apathy and hostility which interferes with the process of "binding up the wounds, not of this or that chance individual, but of an entire race."

Fr. LaFarge once wrote an article entitled "Our Lady and Social Justice," in which he tried to show that Mary knew men and women "not as isolated

spirits, but as members of her nation, needing food and
clothing, medicine, education and civic security." As
the wife of a working man she did not live in the shadows but was socially involved. She was, for this devout
priest, the "supreme witness to the entire drama of the
liberating protest of Jesus" and the "living response to
the far-reaching implications of the ethics that He ex-
emplified and proclaimed." At a time when the attention of many Catholics was riveted on the promises of
Fatima, on Mary-like dresses and green scapulars, Fr.
LaFarge wanted devout Catholics to become involved
in the social order so that Christ's kingdom of justice,
peace, and love would come and the poor would not be
sent away empty. His social consciousness was an important part of his religious faith. The Church has
spoken; her social doctrine must be studied and implemented; that was the leitmotif of his journalistic life.

Around the time that Fr. LaFarge joined the staff of
*America,* communism was being imported into this
country and was beginning to beguile blacks, members
of labor unions, many young people, and a certain
number of intellectuals. He viewed this newly respect-
able social theory as "the greatest evil since the Reformation" and merely "a caricature of Christianity." In
the early thirties he wrote many articles pointing out
the fallacies of Russian Marxism. Communism never
took the center stage in his thought, but for years he
seems to have been conscious of its presence in the
wings.

He refused to attack communists in a negative fashion by indulging in what he called "empty and apocalyptic denunciations." When, for instance, in the 1950s,
Senator Joseph McCarthy was mounting his anti-communist campaign which took on some of the dimensions of a crusade, Fr. LaFarge did not mention the
senator's name even once in the many articles he wrote
at that time.

As early as 1935, this man of sweet reasonableness and sober hope voiced his confidence that ultimately communism would not menace American democracy, either among whites or blacks. He was perceptive enough to see that it could not be imbricated into the structure of the typical American home since, basically, it was not congruent with the American spirit. Nevertheless, he was convinced that communists would resort to relentless propaganda in order to polarize the American community.

Through his regular reading of *Pravda* and *Izvestia* he kept informed on the latest propaganda from Moscow. And he was saddened when he saw how many gullible young Catholics, who had not previously been introduced to Christian ideals of world unity, were being deceived by that propaganda. They were subscribing to communist slogans of world unity and world peace which, he said, "are ours and are Christ's and are *theirs* only because we hide them under a bushel."

Whatever would advance the cause of peace and unity in the world he supported. He was, for instance, one of the founding members of the Catholic Association for International Peace. One of their first meetings was held in the Catholic Club in New York City. A distinguished member of Tammany Hall came into the club that day and, hearing noise upstairs, asked what was going on. Fr. LaFarge told him it was a meeting of the Catholic Association for International Peace. "The Catholic Association for *what?*" groaned this gentleman, "My Lord, what are we coming to?"

World peace and unity, he knew, would never be achieved unless men and women of all shades of belief and unbelief learned to live and talk and work together. Fr. LaFarge was one of the first to engage in ecumenical dialogue. For many years he was an active member of the Conference on Science, Philosophy and

Religion that held its meetings at Columbia University. He was asked to serve for three years on the board of directors of the National Conference of Christians and Jews. *Time* magazine (Mar. 3, 1952) made the observation, "A peculiar gift of Fr. LaFarge's is his ability to get along with his opposite numbers in other religions." And at the Union Theological Seminars, which he also attended regularly, several Protestant theologians claimed that "Fr. LaFarge was one of the few priests with whom a dialogue was possible and fruitful."

As a pastoral theologian he firmly believed that the Eucharist was *the* source and sign of unity among all peoples of the world. Throughout his entire priestly life, therefore, he did much to foster better liturgy. He was a life member of the National Liturgical Conference and read papers at its annual Liturgical Week in many cities across the country. In 1933 he conceived the idea of starting the Liturgical Arts Society. His brother Bancel joined him in the early days and his cousin, Harry Binsse, was the first editor of the quarterly, *Liturgical Arts*. Fr. LaFarge remained chaplain of the group until late in his life. From this organization came the Liturgical Arts Schola, or the Quilisma Club, a chorale which held weekly meetings and prepared a number of Gregorian chant services which they performed in any church or chapel where they could get a hospitable reception.

During his lifetime Fr. LaFarge wrote three books on racism, of which the most important by far was *Interracial Justice: a Study of the Catholic Doctrine on Race Relations*, published in 1937. In the introduction to this book the author's gentle and optimistic approach led him to say that he was not so much trying to persuade people to walk a certain road as he was trying to show them the road he was convinced "they are eventually going to walk on."

A copy of this book came into the hands of Pope

Pius XI, whose encyclical letter, *With Burning Solicitude,* issued a short time before, was the first major official document to confront and criticize racism in Germany. Grievously distressed by the worsening situation in Italy and Germany, the pope was thinking of sending out another warning. Fr. LaFarge helped him in this task.

In the spring of 1938 Fr. Francis Talbot, S.J., editor in chief of *America,* asked LaFarge to go to Budapest and prepare an article on the International Eucharistic Congress to be held there in early June. When the congress was over he made his way to Rome. One day he went out to the pope's summer residence at Castelgondolfo for a general audience. While he was there the pope learned of his presence and asked him to come to his office at noon on June 22. The pope told Fr. LaFarge that his book was the best he had seen on the issue of racism. He then asked him to prepare the rough draft of an encyclical on this subject. "Say simply," the pope told him, "what you would say to the whole world if you yourself were pope." This, he made clear, was to be a secret between the two of them.

In a letter to his superior a few days later Fr. LaFarge said that he was "stunned," as if the rock of Peter had fallen on him. Fearing that the tense political situation in Europe might make it possible for someone to intercept and open his letters he used coded language about the "padlock" imposed by "Buddha." Later he referred to the pope as "Mr. Fisher" (the chief fisherman).

Before the frightened visitor left the Vatican the pope assured him that he would contact the Jesuit General and ask him to provide every assistance. LaFarge asked Fr. Ledochowski that fathers Gustave Gundlach of the Gregorian University and Gustave Desbuquois of *Action Populaire* be allowed to help him.

Throughout the summer these three men sequestered themselves in Paris, at Rue Monsieur, the headquarters of the French Jesuit periodical, *Etudes*. By the
end of the summer they had produced an English,
French, and German edition of a document that boldly
analyzed anti-semitism in Germany and racial prejudice in the United States of America. They assigned it
the provisional title, "The Unity of the Human Race."
On September 20, Fr. LaFarge brought it to Rome, together with some explanatory notes of his own, and
presented it to Fr. Ledochowski. Secrecy has shrouded
its subsequent history.

It appears that Father General did not like the analysis of the political situation in Europe. He kept the
document in his room for a week before passing it
along to a Jesuit on the staff of *Civiltá Cattolica* for
criticism. Not until January 1939, was it placed in the
hands of the aging pope, whose health was fast slip-
ping away. Whether Pope Pius XI ever read the text
seems doubtful. He died on February 10, 1939.

It is significant that this humble priest not only
poured his best efforts into this project which never
saw the light of day, but also that he planned to keep
in utter secrecy both the honor shown him in being
asked to write the encyclical, and the disappointment
he felt when it was not published. Only when he was
in his late seventies did one of his companions on the
staff of *America* discover, quite by chance, that "Uncle
John" (as he was affectionately called at America
House) had prepared the text of an encyclical on
racism.

LaFarge, the teacher, was a man of simplicity, courage and optimism. He had inherited from his father a
"dislike of humbug." He avoided heavy and pedantic
language such as people use who want to enclose themselves behind a wall of specialized jargon. He lamented
the fact that the simplest propositions of justice had to

be proved to Catholics like scientific theorems. And he warned his associates in the interracial movement that they would be like missionaries "conversing with foreign people, bound by tribal customs and taboos." "The idols will bow out," he wrote, "only when people have become sufficiently enlightened to wish to remove them of themselves."

Fr. LaFarge wrote and spoke courageously. He did not want to vest himself in the "silken robes of prudence" and settle for "pussyfooting evasion." He was enough of a realist, however, to recognize that grassroots social reform would not come about without a certain amount of shock. And yet at times he feared that his thoughts would simply ricochet off the foreheads of others. For instance, as early as 1937 he had labeled racism a "sin" and a "heresy." These were strong words. He did not use them again. Rather, he preferred to view racism as a disease which could best be banished by sound education.

And so he gave himself to the task of stemming the tide of racial prejudice with his own distinctive spirit of optimism. At the age of seventy-nine he claimed that his dominant attitude of mind throughout his life, the spirit in which he had tried to approach the vexing problems of the day, was one of "sober hope." He maintained that all members of the Church "by their profession and by their lives should stand out as people of hope." In one of the few passages in his writings where he spoke of the difficulties he had faced, he said:

Indeed, if I were seeking grounds for lost confidence, I could always produce a few examples of my own: cases where one is discouraged by a spirit of bureaucracy, the plague of all institutional life; timidity in high places, or its contrary, rashly bad judgments in meeting the problems of the age.

But he went on immediately to say that the word "Amen," which he chose for the title of his book, *An American Amen*, summed up his philosophy of confidence. He would have nothing to do with angry dissent.

On November 24, 1963, Fr. LaFarge corrected his share of galleys. Then he ate his lunch, went to his room for a nap, and died at 83 years of age with the New York *Times* in his hand and two sets of rosary beads in his pocket. Through his writings and personal contacts for thirty-seven years he had tended his flock with utter fidelity. He had fed the needy, consoled and promoted peace among people who were not as visible as his congregation in Maryland but were just as real for him.

In this century, no Catholic figure, whether moral theologian or member of the hierarchy, rivaled Fr. LaFarge as the chief spokesman for the cause of human rights for blacks. For many years, quite single-handedly, he made the American Church aware of the moral dimensions of interracial problems in this country. Mr. Roy Wilkins, for many years the director of the National Association for the Advancement of Colored People, recalled that in the early days when Fr. LaFarge was establishing the headquarters of the Catholic Interracial Council in New York City, "some of us went to speak, but we stayed to learn at the feet of this selfless man. . . . He left his imprint indelibly on the pattern of race over the nation. . . . He was unquestionably ahead of his time."

It seems almost paradoxical that this unassuming and kindly man should have been a social pioneer. The theology that he learned in the seminary and lived all his life had been written in the penumbral days of the Council of Trent and of the First Vatican Council. He was fiercely loyal to the institutional Church. Yet he was an innovator. Possibly the best way to describe how he accomplished all that he did is to say that he made explicit what was only implicit in the teachings of the Church. What the popes wrote he read with a "third eye." Because of his long years in St. Mary's County, Maryland, his voracious reading, and his almost daily conversations with members of the black race, he was able to see where others could not. Once he recognized a problem, he studied it, and in time spoke out fearlessly and organized programs to solve it. He sensed that the racial situation in this country would change either with or without the Church, and he felt strongly that the Church's solutions, if they were implemented from the grass roots up, were the best.

Even though he spent his entire life working in his native land, he was a missionary. In the words of Dr. George Shuster of Notre Dame, "no other priest of his generation was so effective a missionary to the American people. . . . This was doubtless because he did not seem to be one."

In his autobiography Fr. LaFarge claimed that his own manner was "ordinary"; but like John Berchmans, a Jesuit saint whom he admired and imitated, he did "common things uncommonly well." Whether reading the psalms and prayers of the Church as he strolled back and forth in the courtyard at America House, or celebrating the Eucharist, or participating in banter and story-telling in the community recreation room, or directing retreats, or writing articles and books in his scholarly, yet simple, style, he was a man of extraordinary, if unobtrusive, holiness. Like another John, the Baptist, he constantly prayed "that He may become more and more and I may become less and less." And because God possessed his soul so completely Uncle John became, for many who knew him well, the only authentic saint they had ever met. And he became a prophet whose dreams God brought to rich fulfillment.

# THOMAS MERTON

## Naomi Burton Stone

Thomas Merton was born in Prades, France, on January 31, 1915. His father, Owen Merton, a New Zealander, had gone to Paris to study painting and had there met an American girl, Ruth Jenkins. They had fallen in love and married and moved to the South of France where they could paint and live inexpensively. Owen Merton was a fine artist but it is a hard profession in which to make enough to support a wife and then a son. The First World War was in progress, and that did not make things any easier. Ruth Merton's parents were worried about her and wanted the Mertons to come to Douglaston, Long Island, N.Y., where they lived. So in 1916 the three of them traveled to America and moved into a very small house not far from Ruth's parents. Owen had to support the family by gardening, landscaping and taking care of the gardens of several big houses. In 1918 a second son, John Paul, was born.

Soon after Tom's birth Ruth had started to keep a diary called *Tom's Book*, in which she proudly recorded anecdotes about Tom, his first words, first sentences. Merton remembered her as being quick, nervous, a perfectionist, and saw himself as a dreamy, nonconforming child who was always a disappointment to his mother. Very probably his brother's birth and the inevitable shift of emphasis made him feel out of things, for he certainly was a bright and clever child, and still only a very small boy when tragedy struck the family.

Ruth had cancer and had to go into the hospital, and the boys and Owen moved in with Ruth's parents, the Jenkinses. When Ruth knew that she was dying she wrote a letter to Tom, six years old, telling him she would not see him again. He remembered being given the letter, taking it out-of-doors to read, puzzling out all the words, and feeling his world coming apart. In those days it was thought better to keep children shielded from serious illness and death. The letter must have been a mother's need to speak once more to her older son but to avoid terrifying him by a visit to her in the hospital.

After Ruth's death, Owen and the two boys stayed on with the Jenkinses and Owen was able to devote all his time to painting, sometimes going off on trips and taking Tom along for company. After two years Owen decided to go back to France where he would be better able to keep in touch with the European art critics who were beginning to praise his work. He did not want to leave Tom, and wanted to supervise his education himself, so the two of them set off with the idea of sending for John Paul as soon as they were settled.

Tom's first school was the Institut Jean Calvin in Montauban, but they soon moved on to St. Antonin where Owen decided to design and build a house himself. In the fall, Tom was sent to the boys' *lycée* in Montauban as a boarder, and his memories of this school were bitter. He felt desolate, and pleaded with his father to take him away. He did settle down in the end but was never happy there. The boys tended to be very rough and he had to learn to stand up for himself.

When Owen announced that after all they were going to live in England, Tom was delighted. Owen had relatives and many friends there. When they arrived they stayed in a London suburb with Owen's

Uncle Ben, a retired schoolmaster, whose wife Aunt Maud obviously had a genius for making a child feel understood. But soon Tom was sent off to a small boys' boarding school near London, Ripley Court. He was thirteen and it was discovered with horror that he knew no Latin, and he had the humiliation of joining the lowest class in the school to catch up on a subject that was essential for his future schooling. Tom was always an excellent student, and in the little over a year that he was at Ripley he was able to catch up to his age group and pass the entrance examination for an old but not very well-known school, Oakham, where he would spend four years preparing for college.

While Tom was still at Ripley Court there were indications that all was not well with Owen's health, though no one seemed to know exactly what the trouble was. In the summer of 1929 Owen and Tom traveled to Scotland to stay with friends, but very soon Owen returned to London to enter a hospital, leaving Tom in Scotland. A strange telegram, signed by Owen and saying he was "entering New York harbor" brought Tom hurrying south, where his Uncle Ben met him and announced that his father had a malignant brain tumor. It seemed that Tom was destined always to get the bad news head-on and unadorned. At the hospital Tom found his father lucid but very weak. Surgery was scheduled and Owen asked his son to pray for him.

In the autumn of that year Tom entered Oakham School, and in the summer of 1930 his grandparents, the Jenkinses, came over for a long visit first at Oakham and later in London, bringing John Paul with them. They stayed near the hospital so that they could visit Owen frequently. Tom recalls finding his father unable to speak, though obviously recognizing them all. In his sorrow at his father's helplessness Tom hid his face in the bed-covers and wept, as tears ran down his father's

cheeks. During that summer Tom came to realize that
of them all only his father had any real faith, and he
also sensed that this illness would be long and harrow-
ing for them all.

Tom had another change to contend with when the
Jenkinses and John Paul returned to America. Owen
had seen to it that Tom was baptized in the Anglican
church and had asked a close friend with whom he had
grown up in New Zealand to be his godfather. This
was Tom Bennett (for whom one presumes Tom was
named), who also had traveled to Europe and who by
this time was a successful Harley Street doctor. He was
Owen's age, married but with no children, and very
comfortably off. He offered to let young Tom stay with
them whenever he was in London, and Tom's grandfather Jenkins, who was now the only person in a position of authority in the family, must have thought the
idea a good one. Uncle Ben and Aunt Maud lived a
rather limited life in a London suburb—though their
home was a warm one and Tom considered his aunt an
angel. With them Tom would have had a certain
amount of gentle supervision; but he seems to have
been left very much to himself and treated as if he
were older than he was in fact.

Tom was only sixteen when his father died. His life
was now divided between Oakham School, summer
visits to the Jenkinses in America, and spring vacations
spent in Europe, sometimes with the Bennetts but more
often on his own. It was decided that he should try to
qualify himself for a career in the diplomatic corps,
and Tom Bennett arranged for him to stay with friends
in Germany so that he could study the language. He
was already bilingual in French. The Bennetts were
generous and kind, and certainly encouraged him in his
reading and appreciation of music and the theater, but
there is no doubt Tom rattled about, back and forth

across the Atlantic alone, walking or cycling in Europe unaccompanied.

On one of these walking tours he picked up an infection under a toenail, did nothing about it until he was back at school, and developed general blood poisoning. He was near death and he wanted to die, feeling it would be a suitable climax to his life. But he recovered and turned to studying with so much enthusiasm that he was able to take his entrance examination for Cambridge University at the end of the calendar year and pass it. His reward was another trip—this time to Italy. He traveled by way of the South of France to Florence and then headed for Rome. In the churches he visited as a tourist he found himself strangely drawn to the mosaics, with their pictures of Christ. He began to feel an awareness of the presence of Christ, and one night, in his hotel room, he suddenly felt that his father was actually there with him. Tom looked into his own heart and was disgusted with what he saw, the emptiness and purposelessness of his life. It was a moment of revelation. He began to read the Gospels and now when he entered churches it was to pray in them.

It was a peaceful and joyful time for him. The religious fervor did not die all at once but gradually it began to fade. By the time another American vacation had ended Tom had put on again all the trappings of the sophisticated young fellow about to enter on his college career at Clare College, Cambridge.

Whatever he did at Cambridge, study was clearly the least of it. He writes of drinking, rowdiness, cutting classes, studying subjects of his own choosing rather than what was required of him, and running around with a group of people who did nothing to influence him for good. Friends who knew Tom well in America speak of his fathering a child (who was later killed in the blitz in World War II with the mother), though there does not appear to be any documentation of this.

Whatever the details of his college career in England they obviously displeased Tom himself deeply as he looked back. At the time he ignored his godfather's repeated remonstrances and urgings to settle down, and he was finally summoned to London for an interview that must have been as painful for Tom as for the guardian. The college authorities had made it clear that unless there was a complete change Tom would be asked to leave. His guardian felt that he was a long way from showing qualities that would be useful in the diplomatic corps, and told him that he had better go back to America and his grandparents there. Thinking of the experience he had had in Rome, Tom was completely ashamed of himself and made no defense of his behavior. He knew how much his father had wanted him to be educated in England and how this would have disappointed him. On his way back to America, Tom considered his recent past, wondering if it were not the comparative ease of his upbringing that had made him what he felt himself to be—thoroughly worthless. He had studied Russian Communism (as an extracurricular activity at Cambridge) and now thought perhaps there was no good to be found in the world in which he had grown up.

He moved in with his grandparents on Long Island, enrolled at Columbia University, and made friends there who were to influence the whole rest of his life— Ed Rice, Bob Lax, Sy Freedgood, Bob Gerdy, Bob Gibney, all fellow-students, and two professors, Mark Van Doren and Daniel Walsh. He was nineteen years old. His childhood and adolescence had been filled with tragic loss and there had been precious little of the stability a child needs to develop normally, but he had picked himself up with strength and determination. Now, somehow or other, his openness, sense of fun, his quick wit which made him loved by all who knew him well, had blossomed from the ashes of the Cambridge experience. He had not regained the fervor of the days in Rome—he even had a passing encounter with a group of young communists in New York City—but the seed was in his heart, and beginning to stir.

His grandfather died suddenly. Tom knelt by the bedside and found himself able to pray again. It was perhaps the beginning of the opening of his heart but it was a course in medieval French literature for which he signed up at college that really started the chain-reaction. A book in a store window caught his eye— Etienne Gilson's *The Spirit of Mediaeval Philosophy.* He bought the book and opened it on the train going back to Long Island. To his disgust he saw the book had the Catholic imprimatur—the last thing he wanted to read. He admired a great deal in Catholic culture but abhorred the whole idea of Catholic dogma. Nonetheless he read the book the whole way through and in it he found something which he later felt was the real turning point of his life—the concept that God is the pure act of existing. When he finished the book he found himself wanting to go to church. As a schoolboy he had rejected the "official religion" of the Church of England, but now he decided to visit an Episcopal church on Long Island where his father had once played the organ. He was not a regular attendant and unfortunately the minister seemed less than convincing, so that he soon stopped going.

In his autobiography, *The Seven Storey Mountain,* Merton tells fully and wonderfully of the small component parts of the chain that gradually led him to the day when he decided he must go to Mass, must seek instruction, must ask to become a member of the Catholic Church. Each step seemed connected with the next one—he entered Mark Van Doren's course on Shakespeare by mistake, and stayed in it; some of his friends, Jewish boys, were discussing becoming Catholics, led to the idea by their studies in scholastic philosophy. Ed

Rice was a Catholic. Lax urged him to read Aldous Huxley's *End and Means*, by no means an endorsement of Catholicism, but the author quoted freely from St. John of the Cross, St. Teresa of Avila, and Meister Eckhart. Tom's grandmother had died, too, and John Paul was off at Cornell. Tom spent hours at the old house reading Father Weiger S.J.'s translations of oriental texts. He decided suddenly to write his master's thesis on William Blake, and, through his studies, began to see the absolute necessity for a vital faith, the need to live always in the presence of God. His reading became more and more Catholic, but perhaps the next to final step was his friendship with Sy Freedgood's friend, a Hindu monk, Bramachari, who told Tom he *must* read *The Confessions of St. Augustine* and *The Imitation of Christ*.

One day Tom was reading a life of Gerard Manley Hopkins, whose poetry he loved, and read of Hopkins's writing to Newman, asking about how he could become a Catholic. After a few delays, putting the book down, picking it up again, Tom finally walked down to Corpus Christi Church in New York City and asked Fr. Ford, the pastor, if he could take instruction. On November 16, 1938, he was received into the Catholic Church. He was not a convert given to an excess of "devotions" but a regular Sunday Mass-goer and probably one of the best read, best prepared laymen around.

During the time he was working on his master's thesis, Tom took an apartment in Greenwich Village. He still saw a great deal of his Columbia friends and remembers being startled when Bob Lax, one of the Jewish group (later to become a Catholic), told him that he ought to pray to become a saint—on the grounds that this was the logical objective of all Christians. Outwardly Tom was more interested in sitting up half the night listening to jazz, drinking beer, and dating girls, though he did study hard and was always at work on a novel. One day a group of friends were gathered in Tom's apartment and he stopped conversation by announcing, "I must become a priest."

He did in fact apply to a Franciscan seminary and was accepted for admission in 1940. Before the date arrived he volunteered further information about his past life that made the Franciscans reconsider. Convinced that he did have a vocation, this was a bitter blow to him but he allowed himself only a brief period of unproductive sorrow. He decided to live a much more strict religious life on his own. He attended Mass daily, recited the Office every day as a Third Order Franciscan, and also took a job at St. Bonaventure's, a Franciscan university, in Olean, N.Y., as an instructor in English. That summer he and Rice and Lax shared a cottage belonging to Lax's family in Olean, each of them writing a novel. After hearing Baroness de Hueck (Catherine Doherty) speak of her work in Harlem, he went to work there in Friendship House for a period, wondering if this was to be his lifework.

Somewhere in the back of his mind was a monastery about which Daniel Walsh had told him, asking if such a life would not appeal to him. At that time Tom had said definitely not, it sounded much too austere for him. Now he wrote to ask if he could make a retreat there and was told to come. Compared with the great monasteries of Europe, the abbey of Gethsemani in Kentucky was not physically prepossessing, but Tom found there the inward peace and beauty he had been seeking. He returned to St. Bonaventure for the rest of the year and the start of the fall semester in 1941, but he knew in his heart that it would not be for long. On December 10, 1941, he entered the Trappists, the Order of Cistercians of the Strict Observance, at Gethsemani.

There is no doubt that in doing so Tom expected to

devote the whole rest of his life to prayer and praise of
God through the Divine Office and the Mass and such
manual labor as was assigned to him. He renounced his
name, all his worldly possessions, and, as he thought,
the gift he had for writing. It was not, as yet, a recognized gift but he knew that he was a writer and it was
a sacrifice he was willing to make. He was seeking God
alone, and the idea that he would become a world-
famous author certainly did not occur to him or anyone
else. To those who had read his early, unpublished
novels, it just seemed a pity that the talent should be
wasted, but it was a choice he had clearly made, and
some, at least, never expected to hear from him again.
(Because the Trappists were vowed to silence it was
popularly supposed that they became totally mute
upon entering a monastery. This was, and is, untrue.
While the monks kept a strict silence among themselves, an individual could and did speak to his abbot,
novice master or director, and their voices were used
day and night in the Canonical Hours. Necessary—and
perhaps, at times, unnecessary—conversation between
monks was carried on by sign-language. Today these
rules have been somewhat relaxed.)

Before Tom entered Gethsemani his brother John
Paul had crossed the border and joined the Royal Ca-
nadian Air Force. He kept in touch with Tom by mail
and when he knew he was going overseas he came
down to Kentucky for a visit. With the help of a few
days of intensive instruction from Tom and several of
the monks, John Paul, who was not a total stranger to
Christianity, was prepared for baptism; before he left
the two brothers received Communion together. It was
the summer of 1942. In April 1943, Tom received the
news that John Paul's plane had been shot down in the
North Sea. He had lived a few hours in a survival raft
before being buried at sea by the two survivors. The
last member of Tom's immediate family was gone. One

of Merton's most lovely poems, *For My Brother: Missing in Action 1943*, commemorates his death.

However much Merton expected never to write again, his first abbot, Dom Frederic Dunne, thought otherwise. Frater Louis, as Thomas Merton was now known, was encouraged to write poetry, to undertake some writing and translation the abbot wanted done, and to write his autobiography. Three small books of poetry were published in the 1940s, but it was *The Seven Storey Mountain*, the story of his life from birth to his entrance into the monastery, that catapulted him into fame around the world. The poems had appeared under the name of Thomas Merton, and although it was unusual not to use Frater Louis, his name in religion, Dom Frederic decided that the autobiography also should appear under his lay name. Dom Frederic died before the book was actually published and it was the new abbot, Dom James Fox, who inherited the problems that followed.

The book struck a note that appealed to a whole generation of young men, disillusioned by war, looking for a life in the Spirit. The silent Trappists, withdrawn from the world, were besieged by men wanting to enter the monastery, to visit or perhaps to stay; by people of all ages who wanted to meet this Thomas Merton who had set their hearts on fire. Mail poured in at a rate more usually to be found in Hollywood studios. It was impossible for Merton to answer it all himself, and others were set to replying for him. This did not always please the recipient but it was a necessity and Merton was not at all sorry to be able to get on with his own writing.

Other books followed rapidly. There was a time, of which Merton tells in *The Sign of Jonas*, when he could not write at all, and could not pray at all. Neither feeling is unusual. A writer who has had a great success can be paralyzed with fear of not being able to

write more. In his case it was subconscious, for he was
the most modest of men, really seeming to have no idea
of his enormous popularity and influence on others.
Even in later years when he corresponded with famous
people all over the world, and with ordinary people
who were drawn to God through his writing, he did
not change, was never pompous, never lost the gift of
self-criticism and the ability to laugh at himself and his
circumstances. As to his inability to pray, that, too, is a
rather common phase in the life of anyone dedicated to
a life of prayer, but none the less painful to bear. It
was now that all that had formed him in the difficult
years of his childhood and youth came to his help. He
held on, and gradually regained his inner peace.

There were certainly difficulties for him within the
Trappist order. He longed for an even more quiet life—
there were often more than a hundred monks living in
very close quarters—and he wanted more time for private prayer. In 1951 he was made master of students,
teaching the men who were studying for the priesthood. (He himself had been ordained in 1949.) He
loved the work but it meant more time spent in teaching, less in prayer. Three times he considered the possibility of leaving the Abbey of Gethsemani for a more
rigid life. First of all he thought of leaving it for the
Carthusians, from which he was rather easily discouraged. Then it was to join a new American foundation
of the Camaldolese, and he went into this quite thoroughly. A year after his request for a transfer was refused, he was able to write a friend that he felt much
calmer and happier—had even so far forgotten his devotion to the Camaldolese as to send his first-class relic
of their founder to the laundry in his habit pocket. It
came back unharmed, St. Romuald being "a tough old
bird." The third request was to join a new Benedictine
group, at a time when Merton had many influential
friends in high places, to whom he applied for help.

Permission was necessary because he had taken a vow of stability, to remain in the monastery where he had entered unless sent elsewhere by his superiors. Again his request for a transfer was refused. He was both hurt and angry. At this time other monks were given permission to travel for study, but not Merton. He felt that he was being treated as though he were an irresponsible child, and some of this treatment does seem, in retrospect, to have been over-protective. That was certainly how Merton viewed it and how he wrote of it to a number of friends—letters that reached their destination safely in spite of what was supposedly ironclad censorship.

Twice in his life as a monk a ban on his writing was pronounced, in each case from the abbot general in Rome. The first time was in the 1950s and was concerned entirely with the spiritual life of a son who was cherished by the man who accepted responsibility for Fr. Louis's soul, as opposed to the career of Thomas Merton. The ban was accepted even though there does not seem to have been any actual long gap between his books. What happened at this exact time was that Fr. Louis became novice master at Gethsemani, the position having become vacant. Dom James has said that he was surprised when Fr. Louis volunteered for the job, for he had been listening to his pleas for less community and more solitude, and this was really a full-time job. He agreed at once, probably relieved to see his controversial monk engaged in work for which he was extremely well qualified. His first-class scholarship, his questing mind, his abiding love of God as he sought Him in prayer, would all help to make him outstanding in the position, which he held for ten years. His influence is not only still felt in his own community and its daughter houses, where at least three of his novices are now abbots, but in contemplative orders all over the world. After the Second Vatican Council Merton was in the forefront of monastic reform—not urging people to leave the cloister as some counseled, but looking back in history and finding renewal in the simplicity of the early fathers. His own need for solitude was upheld by the earliest Christian tradition. As he taught his novices, his conferences were written out and mimeographed, became articles, and were later gathered into books.

The ban on writing faded away until the 1960s, when, deeply distressed by the ever-present threat of nuclear war, by evidence of violence and racial injustice, he turned his pen and his influence to support the cause of peace. He wrote articles and had a book accepted for publication; his voice was clear. It disturbed some Catholics, who, albeit of goodwill, felt that a Trappist monk should not be engaging in political arguments. His job was to pray for peace, not to encourage activists. Complaints were made to Rome and the order came down: no more writing on war and peace. Merton was very and outspokenly angry. The temptation to reply that he must follow the dictates of his conscience must have been great. Instead he accepted the will of his superiors: he withdrew the book from publication, explaining to those who looked to his leadership in the peace movement that since he was vowed to obedience he must obey, and that his obedience was in fact a witness for peace. He added that if he disobeyed flagrantly, those who sought to silence him would consider themselves amply justified, and they still would not hear what he was really saying. He continued writing letters to his friends and they were copied and passed around. He even wrote one or two articles under the transparent nom de plume "Benedict Monk." In the end, the ban was forgotten when a new pope, John XXIII, who had sent Merton the stole he wore at his coronation, wrote an encyclical, *Pacem in Terris*.

Through the years Merton had become increasingly well-known not only as an author but as a leader in the civil rights movement, the ecumenical movement, in the study of the techniques of Eastern religions as they might be applied to Christian contemplation, and, as mentioned, the peace movement. None of this ever caused him to abandon the life for which he had come to the abbey. Always the Divine Office, the Eucharist, private prayer and meditation came first. In spite of whatever differences they may have had, Dom James, who was abbot for the longest period of Merton's life as a monk, often said during Merton's lifetime, that he was a monk who strictly adhered to the rule; who, even when they seemed to be in the midst of a head-on collision, never failed to speak with his abbot each day.

In the 1960s Dom James authorized the building of a small cinder-block bungalow where people from the outside world could come and meet with Fr. Louis. At first he spent only days of recollection there, then an occasional night or two, but finally in 1965 he was able to resign as novice master and live full time in the hermitage. Later the building was enlarged, electric power was brought in, and a chapel, a bathroom, and a kitchen were added. To begin with, the heating was by wood fire, lighting by oil lamp, cooking done over the fire, and he really loved the simplicity of that life. Unfortunately his health was not good and it was decreed that he must go down to the abbey, not very far away, for one meal a day. He also had to tote all his water uphill to the hermitage when it was discovered that the stream from which he had been drawing his drinking water was polluted. In return for the amount of time he could be alone, the chance to get up and walk in the surrounding woods before daybreak as he recited the psalms, the hours he could spend in uninterrupted study and writing, the one meal a day at the abbey was a small price to pay.

When he started his full-time hermit life in July 1965, he was intensely happy and eager to make the best possible use of his privacy. He even spoke, himself, about writing far less, really withdrawing, but that was not what happened. For one thing there were continuing requests from the outside world to see him, and Dom James was generous with permissions to visit Merton but not for him to leave the abbey. There was an invitation, for instance, to go with a group of Quakers to Vietnam, which was refused on his behalf. Hermits belonged in hermitages, was the reason given. It rankled—Merton never seemed aware of how famous he was, how much press coverage there would be, and so he felt, again, that he was being treated as a child. But in spite of this treatment he never did decide to leave the monastery, to walk away, and there is absolutely no doubt that he could have done so and that such a course of action was almost certainly proposed to him by friends who could see how his gifts might be well used in the world.

Merton went quite frequently into Louisville—his health was poor throughout his life and he had sessions in hospitals, saw doctors and dentists, called at the library to collect the many books he asked them to get for him, stayed in town for a meal with friends and persuaded them to drop into a bar where he could listen to jazz. In small ways he might have appeared to some as less than a perfect monk. There was a bit of the rebel or perhaps more of a boyish kind of mischief in his nature that made him thoroughly enjoy an escapade.

But the important point to remember is that in the 1960s men and women in religious life were leaving their vocations in large numbers; leaders in the Church, revered by the laity, were publicly stating that they could no longer obey Vatican rulings. No matter what else, Thomas Merton stayed. There must have been times when the pure, secular logic of leaving the cloister and going out to where he could be "really useful" in an active way seemed irresistible. But he resisted, and that is an important part of his Christian witness.

In 1968 Dom James was succeeded as abbot by Dom Flavian Burns, who had been one of Merton's novices. He allowed the hermit to travel, first to the West Coast, then to New Mexico. His journey was not publicized; he gave some conferences, and returned to Gethsemani. Then he was asked to attend a meeting of Asian Christian contemplative superiors in Bangkok and accepted. He was off almost before many of his friends knew of his plans, stopping in Alaska to consider the possibility of a hermitage there, while still remaining a monk of the Gethsemani community. He visited India, to speak at an ecumenical gathering, to visit and talk with Buddhist monks who had been exiled from Tibet, and to have three meetings with the Dalai Lama. After a brief stay at a tea plantation he went to Ceylon and thence to Bangkok. From photographs taken along the route it is clear that he was well and happy—he looked immensely fulfilled. He had set out on the trip as a pilgrim, a student, not as a preacher. His few letters back and the journals he kept en route indicate that he had learned a lot, perhaps not least that in order to appreciate one's immediate surroundings it is necessary, sometimes, to leave them and gain perspective. The day of the Bangkok address was a great one for him. His was the main speech and it was enthusiastically received. Everyone talked later about his enthusiasm, his brilliance, his openness and charm. A stranger who met him in an Indian airport and spent three hours with him later wrote the abbey of the extraordinary impression this man had made on him, his feeling that here was someone very close to God.

A few hours after the Bangkok talk, Thomas Merton went to shower and take a siesta. A faulty electric fan that he must have been trying to move fell on him, and he was electrocuted. He was found only when he failed to show up at the next meeting and people went to look for him. The date was December 10, 1968, twenty-seven years to the day from his entry into the abbey of Gethsemani.

The young man who had given up the world for the cloister, expecting to live in obscurity, was so well-known that the story of his death was reported on the front page of the New York *Times*. The body of the monk who had worked for peace and condemned war so firmly was flown back to the United States on an Air Force plane which was carrying the bodies of soldiers killed in Vietnam. Instead of the usual private burial, the monks of Gethsemani opened their doors to a large group of his friends, rich and poor, black and white, famous and unknown. For that day the enclosure rule was lifted so that they could follow his body to the monks' cemetery, where it lies close to the walls of the basilica.

Great gifts carry great responsibility. Thomas Merton was an exceptionally gifted person. He was a fine writer, artist, photographer, teacher, spiritual adviser, leader, and, perhaps above all, friend. He did not negate his gifts but had the true humility to recognize them and acknowledge their source. He could have used them for his own gain or glorification but he never did. He retained his great sense of humor and fun to the end. From the time he realized that he sought God and God alone, he never turned back. He endured. He was fifty-three years old when he died, yet his abbot Dom Flavian was able to say of him, expressing what the community felt: "This was a younger Brother, even a boyish Brother, one who could have lived a hundred years without growing old." His love of God and his great faith live on in the hearts not only of those who knew him but in countless others who have read what he had to say on so many subjects, on so many levels, reaching people of all kinds of backgrounds.

There is a passage in the Epistle of St. James that seems to speak of Thomas Merton: "Consider yourselves fortunate when all kinds of trials come your way, for you know that when your faith succeeds in facing such trials, the result is the ability to endure."

## A PERSONAL NOTE

I met Thomas Merton in 1940 when he brought a novel into the literary agency where I worked. We had a certain amount in common—we were both English, we were both (obviously) interested in writing, and when I read this first novel at least part of it described a background that was familiar to me too: nightclubs, jazz, and according to today's standards some very mild hell-raising. I loved the book, which was wild and whacky and funny, and I tried to sell it. To no avail. We met now and again and Tom brought in a second novel, which I also tried to sell but withdrew after some resounding negative response. Tom destroyed the first of these books, before he entered the monastery; the other was published just after his death and is called *My Argument with the Gestapo*. I had no idea that Tom was a Catholic, much less that when I met him he must have been contemplating making a serious commitment to religious life. He went off to teach at St. Bonaventure in western New York. We corresponded until I returned the second novel to him. Then Bob Lax came to see me, bringing the news that Tom had entered the Trappist Order in Kentucky. It certainly sounded to me as though he would never be heard from again. I had thought he had promise but if

he insisted in shutting himself up in some medieval
monastery it was his life. . . .

But I did remember exactly who he was when
Thomas Merton, now Frater Louis, wrote me in 1947
to ask if he could submit the typescript of his autobiography. I said yes, and he sent it along. It was called
*The Seven Storey Mountain* and it did not take a great
deal of perspicacity to pronounce it a readable, saleable
book. Tom even told me where to send it—to Bob
Giroux at Harcourt Brace & Company, who found it ex-
ceedingly publishable. For the next twenty-one years I
was in touch with Tom, mostly by letter, but with a
few visits to the abbey of Gethsemani thrown in, not so
much as editor, for he needed very little if any help in
that direction, but as mediator in his somewhat tangled
publishing affairs. Tom was forever "just giving this
fellow a tiny pamphlet" which would turn out in print
to be a book, when he already had two excellent publishers, Bob Giroux and James Laughlin of New Directions, with whom he had contracts. It seemed to me
that whenever I did go to see Tom it was to straighten
out some tangle, often connected with foreign publishers. It was the kind of situation that was bound to
result in either disenchantment or real friendship, and
given Tom's sense of humor, his contriteness—"now,
what writing do I have to confess to you . . ." he
wrote me, once—it ended in a lasting bond.

I was not a Catholic when I first read *The Seven
Storey Mountain* and not for some years after, though
it certainly was part of my first steps in that direction. I
think that I probably had in some ways a better relationship with him, certainly gave him better objective
advice, in those days. When I became a Catholic I
started expecting Tom to be a saint, on my terms; halo,
piety, no word lacking in charity. I was disappointed,
and Tom found it more than trying. He bemoaned the
high expectations his friends had of him. Looking back

I can see that I really was a prig, busily observing all abbey rules—if I was allowed to drive Tom to Louisville to the dentist, to the dentist we went and no sidetrips to small French restaurants. Visits always began so well but often ended in arguments, and I have heard Tom's voice on a tape saying: "Naomi Burton arrives tomorrow. I do hope we shan't fight too much. (sigh) But I love her very much and she loves me too in her damn mothering way." And that does about sum it up. Perhaps it is just special pleading to say that a friendship with no misunderstanding, never a cross word, is likely to be on the pallid side; but I believe our disagreements, which never were serious enough to break off the relationship, did build up something very special to us both. In the midst of a storm Tom could be so outrageously funny that one just had to laugh and make up.

It is thirteen years since he died. A great deal has been written about him and will continue to be written, but each time I go back to one of his "journal books," *The Seven Storey Mountain, The Sign of Jonas* or *Conjectures of a Guilty Bystander* (and one should probably add *The Secular Journal, My Argument with the Gestapo,* and any of his poetry since that shows much of what I think of as "the *real* Tom"), I hope that whatever has been written about him will lead people to read what he had to say himself, either in the field of spiritual guidance or the books that are just about his life, his thoughts, that speak to so many different kinds of people. My favorite spiritual book is *Thoughts in Solitude,* mostly for itself, but a little bit because I have a letter from him saying that maybe we should withdraw it, because he had come to the conclusion that it was no better than the kind of spiritual writing he often deplored. I happened already, in typescript, to have formed a deep attachment to *Thoughts in Solitude* and said NO loud and fast.

I read over recently a little piece I wrote right after Tom's death when, in a sense, I had a clearer picture of his life than it is possible to have today. At that time I said: "Contrary to some concepts of holiness, my idea of the raw material of sanctity is not a thick river of molasses oozing sluggishly towards Heaven. It is fire and passion and pain and frustration and failure and renewed effort." I was pleased to find that the quality I picked out then was the one that I still see as central to his whole life, the virtue of heroic endurance, that endearing ability to be able to see the absurd in life even when it was filled with pain, the absolute faithfulness to his lifelong search for God alone.

# PADRE PIO

## John McCaffery

*Nil novi sub sole.* "There is nothing new under the sun." This piece of concentrated Mediterranean wisdom is as true today, despite our computerized context, as it was when it was first uttered. The title of the present book in its own specific context obliquely implies it. And Padre Pio, the stigmatized bilocationist saint of our times, was and is its living testimony. —Let me try to explain.

We tend, I think, to have a distorted view of the past. The characters by which it is peopled become flat figures, like two-dimensional pictures in a book. We very often forget that when they were acting their parts the play was in progress for them then just exactly as it is for us now. They were alive, not knowing what the morrow would bring or how their actions and their lives would finish. Above all, they were modern men and women, the latest arrivals on the earth, with the past behind them and the future before them, precisely as we, who are speeding towards the past of our successors, find ourselves playing our parts today. —It is a thought worth keeping in mind.

But, despite its truth, is it possible still to assert, with our possession of the micro-chip and with men hitting golf balls on the moon, that nothing new has appeared under the sun? Most assuredly it is. Very importantly, the kings and shapers of the world's destiny, the new-

born children, are still being born as they were at the
beginning of time; and the contemporary baby, with its
embryo intellect, willpower, and seemingly endless
storehouses of memory and imagination, is the same
model as was its primitive predecessor. The baby is
now as then greater in his or her capacity for thought
and free reasoned action than the earth, the planets,
and the fixed stars, for these in their inertness do but
follow a pattern established for them and imposed.
—All that has altered is the evolving material background and the increased sensitivity of the infant's
bodily instruments.

But then, is not the alteration of the surrounding
background something new? Not really. One cannot
describe as new something which has always been
there. It may be new to our experience, like coming
across growing cocoa-nuts for the first time; but our
misguided pride in our present era of technological
progress might be salutarily tempered were we to recognize that every so-called invention, from the wheel
through steam and combustion engines to the unleash-
ing of nuclear energy, is merely the progressive discovery and exploitation of properties in matter which have
always been there for us to find. In other words, far
from worshiping man, as is the present fatuous custom,
each new discovery should find us on our knees, at least
metaphorically, in awe and admiration for the vast intelligence and power—and I speak by analogy—which
created man in all the wonder of his gifts and put at
his disposal the incredible treasure house of the earth
and all the universe of which it forms part.

These considerations I would hope to be not just a
development of the initial background thesis that there
is nothing new under the sun, but also by association,
as indicated, a relevant introduction to that twentieth
century man called Padre Pio, spiritual son of St.
Francis, observer of his thirteenth-century rule and

wearer of his rough medieval habit, to whom during his lifetime modern men and women came literally in millions seeking solace, enlightenment, and strength of soul and body, and at whose tomb they now come, still in their millions, to pray. He was and is the living proof that God being God, and man being man, inheritor and steward of God's creation, that sanctity which expresses the deep intelligent assessment of such a relationship is as topical and as rational today as it was in the time of St. Francis or indeed at any other time in human history. And if I begin this account of him with such a wide, almost metaphysical preamble, it is because he can be properly understood only within a fresh view of our daily world and of the awesome but largely overlooked structures and forces which constitute and govern it.

Other men and women can be fitted, as it were, into our normal viewing of the world in action, where people may be seen to do good or evil in greater or less degree. But to understand Padre Pio and all that is known of him we must shed the scales from the eyes with which we normally look, and see the most ordinary things in life as the wonders that they really are, not even infinitely self-producing items, which by their finiteness they cannot be, but the amazing products of that power and intelligence already referred to, which transcends all our human understanding. Perhaps in our accurate vision of the ordinary we shall be able then to grasp and accept what for us still remains the extraordinary.

Who and what was Padre Pio? The story of his life in its chronological sequence is a simple one. He was born at the end of the last century, in the year 1887, at Pietralcina, in one of the poorest, most barren and backward areas of southern Italy. His parents were peasants, so poor that his father, Orazio Forgione, twice had to cross the Atlantic for a time to find the means to support his family. One of his two sons, Francesco, showed signs of deep piety at an early age and when he was fifteen years old entered a Franciscan Capuchin monastery as an aspirant to the priesthood. His health was poor and for some time he had to interrupt his studies and the severe life of a Capuchin novice, but eventually he was ordained. His health, however, remained fragile. Pulmonary tuberculosis was diagnosed, and for between five and six years he performed his priestly duties chiefly from his own home; but during that same period, despite his state of health, he immersed himself in a life of extreme asceticism and continuous contemplation. After a spell of parish work in the town of Foggia, he was transferred in the year 1918 to the small monastery of Santa Maria delle Grazie about a mile from the village of San Giovanni Rotondo, some two hundred miles south of Rome, in isolated mountain country that in those days was reached only by rough cart tracks. Here one might say that he was buried from the world, since he never emerged again from the confines of its monastic seclusion right up to his death in 1968. The annals of the Capuchin order in Italy contain other similar records of holy men who now rest forever in tranquil anonymity.

What then was different about Padre Pio that he should have drawn men to him as he did and that his name should have become known and venerated across the entire face of the earth? Different people may give varying interpretations of the phenomena which took place in that little monastery to make it a world beacon; but about the phenomena themselves there can be no doubt, for they were witnessed, sifted, and experienced in their effects by large numbers of intelligent persons. Not only that, but the Church authorities were so reluctant to accept their authenticity that for ten entire years, in the fear that they were manifestations of autosuggestion, hysteria, deliberate deception, or even diabolical possession, Padre Pio was cut off from outside contact, even by letter, and he was not allowed to confess penitents or to say Mass in public.

The Church has always preferred to have her saints dead, so to speak, because so long as they are alive they have free wills and are subject, at least theoretically, to the possibilities of weakness or error; and in this specific case, against the emotional backdrop of an uneducated populace in the region concerned, they were terrified of an eruption of superstitious, falsely based religious fervor. So the phenomena attaching to Padre Pio, in order to be recognized as real and authentic, not only had to contend with a cynical, sometimes derisive public, but had to overcome the distrust and even one might say the distaste of the heads of his own order and of the Vatican.

I have to confess that for roughly a decade after first learning of Padre Pio I was myself wholly cynical, remaining unmoved by anything I read and even by the testimony of respected friends. The only written work which eventually made some impression upon me was a volume compiled by an eminent Roman physician, last of those entrusted with a medical examination of Padre Pio's stigmata. He had begun as a contemptuous unbeliever in the seriousness of what he had been asked to investigate, but in more than two hundred pages covering a two-year period he gave a detailed account of his experiments to find a humanly explicable cause for those stigmata, and ended with a confession of failure and the conclusion that their origin and continuance could be ascribed only to benignly preternatural intervention. He became a devoted disciple of the man whose wounds and whose psychology he had coldly, methodically, and often most harshly probed.

But my real conversion and conviction, my light on the road to Damascus, came only when I reluctantly consented to go down to San Giovanni with an old friend and met the man himself. It was, I have to say, the nearest thing I could imagine to meeting Christ; and in his presence all the reluctance and quasi-hostility fell away, and all the incredible phenomena became easily and even logically acceptable.

What were these phenomena? In the first place there were the stigmata, which is to say the five open and perpetually bleeding wounds in his body corresponding to those of the crucified Christ. The description of their genesis is as follows.

Mainspring of Padre Pio's spiritual life lay in the contemplation of the sufferings and death of Jesus. He had been most profoundly moved not only by these tremendous things in themselves and by their connotations, but by the fact that Jesus in that hour of supreme trial for his humanity had been abandoned even by his closest followers and left to suffer all that he did alone. Then one day realizing and pondering the fact that for God there was not the same succession of past, present, and future as for us, he understood that his own sufferings, deliberately sought after and willingly accepted now, could actually be made concomitant with those of his Master then, thus ensuring that he was no longer left alone and forsaken. He begged to be allowed to suffer as much as was humanly possible without dying; and, quite simply, his request was granted.

For some years he had experienced at his home, amidst a host of other and varied tribulations, accepted or self-imposed, what are known as the hidden stigmata or intense pains at the points of Christ's wounds without any visible sign; and then, after he had joined the monastery at San Giovanni Rotondo, he was found unconscious one day before the crucifix in the church gallery where the friars conducted their community prayers and where he himself went often to pray and meditate. To his intense embarrassment, he and the friar who helped him to his cell discovered that his hands and feet were completely transfixed and bleeding. And these wounds, as well as another in his side leading to the heart, bled continuously and freshly as though newly inflicted for all of fifty years, disappearing gradually only some few weeks before his death. It was indeed a truly remarkable phenomenon.

But there was another one even more remarkable. In the two-thousand-year history of the Catholic Church there have been few people officially recognized as genuine stigmatists. But to an even smaller number, less than can be counted on one hand, has been accorded recognition of the gift of bilocation, or the possibility of being in two places at the same time—which, of course, sounds absolutely preposterous.

But preposterous or not, "There are more things in heaven and earth, Horatio. . . ." Benedetto Croce, the Italian philosopher, once expressed this very succinctly when in reply to a question on a very different topic he said: "Believe in the Evil Eye? Of course not! How could one? —But, mind you, it exists!" And so it was with Padre Pio's bilocation; for, mind you, it existed.

How can one actually assent to such a thing? Well, as a Catholic, without too much difficulty. Most Catholics do not even consciously realize that they accept not just bilocation but the most widespread multilocation when they believe that Christ exists through transubstantiation in every one of their church tabernacles throughout the world; and that if a hundred people receive Holy Communion, Christ in his whole person and personality comes to each one of that hundred under the appearance of bread. They would, of course, point out that Christ was God. Quite so; but without our comprehending the mechanics of this, so to speak, as well as we do those of transubstantiation, it is not inconceivable that what God can do of and for himself

he may well delegate exceptionally to one of his creatures.

That, anyhow, is the theoretical rationalization of it.
It deals with the possibility of the phenomenon's taking
place. But there is the more immediate and important
question of its actuality.

Though few of us have been to the Fiji islands, on
the basis of human testimony in all its ramifications we
have the complete certainty of their existence. Through
a similar process we are absolutely sure that there once
was a character called Julius Caesar. A vast number of
our personal certainties are reached by the same
means. And in the case of Padre Pio's bilocation the
weight and character of such human attestation can
leave no doubt whatsoever about the hard fact of it,
even for persons not as materially close to the evidence
and circumstances of it as was the present writer.

Finally, for those not persuaded of the possibility, let
them ask themselves, for instance, whether they can
describe the appearance of their ideas and judgments,
or the dimensions of the images that fill their imagina-
tions and memories, or where these are kept when they
are not being called up and observed, and they will
perhaps realize that in their uncomprehending acceptance of the ordinary by reason of its being there, the
acceptance also of the extraordinary by reason of its
likewise established existence is not as harebrained as it
might at first sight have seemed.

These phenomena of the stigmata and bilocation I
have wished to deal with first because of the credibil-
ity-resistance which they were obviously bound to in-
spire in persons unversed in ascetical history, not
convinced of an omnipotent legislator capable of re-
arranging his laws, or simply unaccustomed to looking beyond the superficial appearances of things. But
they were very far from being the only phenomena
which made of the little monastery of San Giovanni

what I have not been alone in terming a world beacon.

From Padre Pio's complete immolation of himself there flowed out a multiplicity of other gifts. He possessed the most astonishing insight into men's minds, into their backgrounds and circumstances, into their future. The knowledge that he showed of all that was taking place in the world without benefit of media of any kind was extraordinary. Sometimes in an effort to lighten life for him I would bring up extraneous subjects to discuss, and to this day I remember the grasp he showed both of situations and personalities in international politics, and the extreme perceptiveness of some of his assessments. He not only healed men morally, which might be called his chief aim with them; the number of those he healed physically, not only directly at San Giovanni but indirectly elsewhere, is legion—even when confined to those cases which are formally attested. To some of these healings I was witness, and in my own personal instance I calculate that so far he has obtained for me more than a score of years of borrowed time. —Last but very much not least I would place among his outstanding attributes that of his complete normality in makeup and behavior, which for a man endowed with such marvels and unceasingly surrounded by suppliant and respectful devotees was truly noteworthy.

On top of that there was the wonder of what one might call his life-style. For fifty years in which he bore the sufferings described, walking around on those pierced feet and using those pierced and agonizing hands, he ate as much daily as would sustain a bird—generally a forkful of vegetables or pasta—and this because he was constrained by obedience to join the other friars at their midday meal. His drinking too was absolutely minimal; and altogether I think it would be fair to say that the strongest of ordinary men, living the life he lived, and undergoing the suffering and loss of blood he underwent, would have been dead of exhaustion, malnutrition, anaemia, and dehydration within a matter of months—even without all the rest.

When I first knew him, sixteen years before his death, his public day began at five o'clock each morning with the celebration of Mass. This, for him the very real renewal of the sacrifice of Calvary, was the central point of his existence, and he had already spent something like two hours preparing for it. It was also the highlight of the day for the pilgrims, and the church was packed with people old and young, Italians and foreigners, who had risen around four o'clock and come up through the darkness to follow that Mass with a rapt fascination. It lasted for about an hour and a half, and it could be said that having seen his Mass, one had then really begun to get a true understanding of the person of Padre Pio himself.

There was nothing theatrical about it. There was drama, yes, for one could see at times that the celebrant was viewing and experiencing things which were hidden from his congregation; but it was subdued, contained; it formed part of his total, reverent identification with the mystery in which he was participating; and the timbre of his voice was always low and lacking in tension. What did come through it was his acute awareness of the presence of God, his deep and humble veneration, and on the part of the onlookers the clear realization of his own offering of himself, of his personal immolation. No one there had ever before seen a Mass such as this one now being celebrated on the barren slopes of the Gargano by a lowly monk; and if one took away nothing else from San Giovanni, the memory of that Mass would have been more than enough, for in the course of it some of his own deep awareness of its significance rubbed off on the rest of us; and in an age blinded by human arrogance and pride we understood that the miraculous powers possessed by Padre Pio had their source in his realization of the utter subservience and dependence of man upon him who had created him.

During the day that followed his hour of thanksgiving, begun in the sacristy and concluded whilst another friar said Mass in the monastery oratory, he had times that were reserved for private devotion and meditation, times during which Our Lady's rosary was seldom absent from his hands. He had duties to carry out as spiritual director of the community. He distributed Communion to the people during the morning and gave public benediction of the Blessed Sacrament in the church during the afternoon. He was under perpetual earnest assault by the throngs of suppliants who came to him from every corner of the globe and who waited his passing for a word or blessing in church and sacristy, in the corridor communicating with the monastery, in the monastery itself, and sometimes, if occasion justified it, in his cell. —But most of all he spent long and strenuous hours every day, every week, every month, every year, without break or relaxation, in the confessional.

There he sat, in the stifling heat of summer and the freezing cold of winter—for San Giovanni has both extremes—as he listened to the tales of human weakness and misery, comforting, consoling, counseling, strengthening, inspiring, and sending men and women back into the battle of life with a new resolve, a new vision, and a new ally. There too were mostly brought to him the unending moving requests for help in bodily ills or adverse circumstances. And no pilgrim in good faith went empty-handed away, even if sometimes the grace he received was not the one he had sought, for there too Padre Pio's insight obviously played its part. The confessional was his chief channel of contact and of assuagement with his fellow man.

And then, besides all that, for the last twenty or so

years of his life there was the hospital, the great pale, beautiful hospital, whose constructors and then administrators he had to find all the time necessary to instruct and advise them.

When first he mooted the idea of building a large hospital to serve the needs of that poverty-stricken area in the primitive and isolated surroundings of the monastery, it could only appear to be a quixotic, impossible dream. There was just nothing on which to base a reasonable projection: no communications, no infrastructure, no qualified labor, no seeming prospect of qualified staff, no finance. The scheme's lack of feasibility was compounded when he chose a degreeless architect to design it in all its complexity and a country doctor to supervise its construction. But today there it stands, a thousand-bed hospital possessing the most up-to-date specialized sectors and equipment, with a highly competent staff of doctors and nurses, and with all the ancillary services, facilities and communications which an efficient hospital demands.

Its inauguration, which I attended, was made the occasion for an international cardiological conference; and the greatest names of the day in that field attended it. The men I saw most of were Olivekronen from Sweden, Paul White (President Eisenhower's consultant) and Wangensteen from the States, and Evans from London. None of them was a Catholic, but all of them were deeply and sincerely impressed, not just by that amazing hospital, but a great deal more by the extraordinary, saintly man behind it all. Paul White, most courteous of men, was so moved that on greeting Padre Pio with the rest of his colleagues I remember he finished his little congratulatory speech with the uncharacteristically gauche phrase ". . . and congratulations, Father, on your wounds"! Evans said they were the most fascinating three days of his whole life. And afterwards during the papal audience that followed the conference I listened to White singing the praises of Padre Pio and his hospital to Pius XII and suggesting that a world centre for psychosomatic studies be set up at San Giovanni Rotondo.

There we have a very fundamental picture. In the confessional and the hospital are to be found the essential symbols and synthesis of Padre Pio's life. And that the confessional, with all its aura of antiquity is, like sainthood, part and parcel of our day, may be demonstrated by the highly geared professional competence of the hospital, and by the fact that hub and centre of them both was one and the same person.

It is against the whole background which I have tried to sketch in, both abstract and concrete, that I should like Padre Pio and the phenomena which invested him to be seen. Certain abstract considerations which I have adduced may well lead any reasonable person to conclude that not only the stigmata and bilocation but all the other miracles which poured out from San Giovanni Rotondo for almost half a century were less remarkable than our persistent blindness in not recognizing the staggering, gargantuan miracles of intelligence and device that make up ourselves and that material world which for a time we have inherited. It should also be clear that not only was Padre Pio himself a very normal contemporary human being with a warm, compassionate, and intelligent personality, but that if millions of people went down to see him and came away wholly impressed and often transformed, they could not all have been, and in the specific examples given above most certainly were not, either fanatics or simpleminded.

I spoke of the miracles that poured out from San Giovanni, which is to say those worked through his intercession upon other people. They were innumerable; and as well as having been myself healed of serious cardiac and circulatory ills contracted during the war years, I saw a number of the more striking miracles at close quarters.

I can still see the rugged face of the ex-communist taxi driver from Tuscany as with tears in his eyes he watched Padre Pio leave the sacristy after Mass, still and always walking upon those pierced feet, and murmured to me, "Look at him! Goodness itself walking!" Padre Pio had appeared to him at his home near Florence and reprimanded him severely for his drunken ill-treatment of his wife. Incredulous that this could really have happened, he had stubbornly driven all the way down to the little monastery in a spirit of disbelief and challenge, and had soon found himself upon his knees in Padre Pio's confessional. He left it one of Padre Pio's most loyal and constant devotees.

Another ex-communist I met at San Giovanni was former editor of one of the party's newspapers. To him Padre Pio had appeared when he was in the act of committing suicide and taking his little daughter with him. My conversations with him were not only moving; they were on occasion also amusing, for he had retained his communist vocabulary, and in speaking, for example, of the Church in its human organizational form, he would refer to it as "the *Apparat*"! He told me that after his conversion he had—with typical application—read many lives of saints to find out what it was essentially that constituted sainthood. "I came to the conclusion," he said, "that a man was the more a saint the more he resembled Christ. And that is what binds me ever more closely to Padre Pio: his tremendous Christlikeness." —His application had not been in vain.

To my old friend Giovanni Gigliozzi, writer, journalist, and broadcaster, Padre Pio had appeared in dramatic fashion in Rome's Broadcasting House. Afterwards, when they met again in the monastery and Giovanni thanked him for his intervention, he smiled, and displaying that sense of humor which, despite his sufferings, was never far absent from him, he jocularly remarked: "Ah, these hallucinations!"

The friar with whom I was for years in closest friendship at San Giovanni was Father Dominic, a charming and holy American whose beaming smile reflected all the kindliness of his nature. Not only had Padre Pio cured him of cancer; he had assisted Father Dominic's father in bilocation on his deathbed in Milwaukee.

Three men whom I got to know at San Giovanni came together to my office one day in Milan. One of them had been dying of throat cancer, able to talk only in a barely audible whisper. He was now speaking in his normal robust voice and (I regret to say!) smoking a succession of strong American cigarettes. Second of the three had been blind, with eyes so eaten by disease that they looked like shrivelled dried peas in his head. Those same eyes, perfectly re-formed, were now regarding me across the desk. But there was an interesting inset to his story.

When he had implored Padre Pio to pray that his sight might be restored and had received an affirmative promise, he had added "even if it be only from one eye." When he returned three weeks later, weeping with joy, to thank his benefactor for the incredible transformation, he was asked "And so you now see again perfectly?" "Yes," he replied, "from this eye, not from the other one." Padre Pio shook his head reproachfully. "Let that be a lesson for you," he said. "Never put limitations on God. Always ask for the big grace."

As I finished questioning these two and listening to the detailed accounts of their cures, the third man spoke. He was Carlo Campanini, then Italy's foremost humorous stage actor, and he observed with some conviction that neither of them had been vouchsafed as big a cure as he had. The smoker asked him with surprise what had been his ailment. "You, my friend, had cancer of the throat," said he. "That was child's play. I had cancer of the soul. It needs, believe me, a miracle much more difficult to achieve." And to prove it he told us the story of *his* healing.

The list of astonishing happenings with whose participants I was in direct friendly relations and of whose veracity there could be no doubt could be continued; and there is an even longer list of similar or still more astonishing episodes of which I had indirect but wholly convincing knowledge.

There were, too, happenings which seemed at first so outlandish that, even with all the evidence of the miraculous which I had witnessed or experienced, they appeared to me to be pure Mediterranean legend. I am thinking especially of the story of Padre Pio's appearing in the sky during the last war and turning back an American bombing mission due to drop its bombs near San Giovanni Rotondo. That, as I say, I took to be heroic folklore in the making—until the day when the leader of the squadron in question surfaced personally in the course of a trip from the States to revisit an old friend he had first encountered away up there in the Italian clouds, of whose existence he had previously been entirely unaware. It was no legend; it was just another of those facts of which I have now been attempting to convince other people, and he recounted it in detail to Lord Eldon, sometime lord in waiting to Queen Elizabeth, when they met in a rail compartment on their common journey from Rome down to San Giovanni Rotondo.

It is being asked everywhere at the moment how long it will be before the Vatican canonizes Padre Pio and thus officially proclaims him to be a saint. It should not be too long, I would think, for the astonishing happenings have not ceased with his death. Not only have I been given circumstantial reports of quite a number of extraordinary physical cures obtained after requests for his intercession, but in one, of which I shall now tell, I was actually closely involved.

Going into a local bank one morning I was approached by a member of the staff. She said she had read my book, *Tales of Padre Pio*, and she wanted to know whether I possessed anything which had belonged to him because her sister was going blind and wanted to touch her eyes with it. (This will certainly sound to some like benighted superstition, but it is something I have discussed, I hope rationally, in my book; and again, for how much more proof can one ask than the evidence of one's eyes—or in the present instance of someone else's?)

I enquired what was the nature of her sister's eye affliction. She answered that it seemed the eyes were perishing from behind and that the specialists to whom she had been brought had said there was nothing they could do. I told her that on the following Sunday a lady who had a scarf of Padre Pio's was coming from Dublin to Donegal to give a lecture and show a film on him, and that if she brought her sister along I would introduce her.

She brought her, and I found it terribly pathetic in talking to this pretty youngster of eighteen or nineteen years of age to see her affected by a continuously recurring blink of the eyelids. I introduced her to the lecturer, and with reverence she made the sign of the cross and touched her eyes with the scarf.

Some six weeks later in the course of another visit to the bank I was informed by her sister that the blink had completely gone, that the specialists to whom she had been brought back could find no trace of her disease, and that she had now begun a secretarial course. Since then she has been employed for almost two years in another bank, and she had her last satisfactory eye check three weeks ago.

Now this is perhaps not as striking or conclusive a cure as the well-known one worked by Padre Pio at San Giovanni upon a young Italian girl born without pupils in her eyes who today is walking around, seeing, though still without pupils; but it took place in a very ordinary contemporary setting, and it seems to me to be a very clear indication that, whether it be up in the sky, or in Tuscany, Milwaukee, or Donegal, the world today is still God's world in which he tries at times to recall to us the wonder of the laws on which his creation rests by every so often suspending them.

If we think well on it, I believe we shall have to admit that none of the happenings I have described is half as extraordinary as the fact of which I have spoken that we remain mentally blind before the marvels constituting and surrounding us—marvels like a normal eye, or a tooth, or the humblest sparrow hopping on a window sill, or a field of growing grass or corn; or that the appearance amongst us of a man like Padre Pio should have made, not so much, but really so little impact upon his fellowmen.

When Francis Thompson, the English poet, wrote the stanzas entitled *The Kingdom of God* which were found among his papers after his death, he might easily have been expressing the reactions of some pilgrim returning from a visit to San Giovanni Rotondo; and such is their relevance that I make no apology for embellishing this chapter by quoting them in full:

### The Kingdom of God

#### 'In No Strange Land'

O world invisible, we view thee,
O world intangible, we touch thee,
O world unknowable, we know thee,
Inapprehensible, we clutch thee!

Does the fish soar to find the ocean,
The eagle plunge to find the air—
That we ask of the stars in motion
If they have rumour of thee there?

Not where the wheeling systems darken,
And our benumbed conceiving soars!—
The drift of pinions, would we hearken,
Beats at our own clay-shuttered doors.

The angels keep their ancient places;—
Turn but a stone, and start a wing!
'Tis ye, 'tis your estrangèd faces,
That miss the many-splendoured thing.

But (when so sad thou canst not sadder)
Cry;—and upon thy so sore loss
Shall shine the traffic of Jacob's ladder
Pitched betwixt Heaven and Charing Cross.

Yea, in the night, my Soul, my daughter,
Cry,—clinging Heaven by the hems;
And lo, Christ walking on the water
Not of Gennesareth, but Thames!

Saints are Now. And that Now has meant, means, and will mean yesterday, today, and tomorrow; for all men have always had Now.

Looking at our Now of today, it is clear that more than most of our predecessors we have a lot of crying and clinging to do; because despite all the highly evolved, up-to-date means we possess of observing it, there is just no doubt that we have sadly missed the many-splendored thing; and the fruits of our inadvertence lie all around us. Half the world is enslaved literally, the other half is in great part slave to myopic, disintegrating hedonism, and we stand teetering on the brink of nuclear self-destruction.

Perhaps through Padre Pio, God has been making a last attempt to tell us that he can do extraordinary things also for us if we do but open our clay-shuttered eyes and ears to his creation and give him the chance.

# EDITH STEIN

*Philip J. Scharper*

August 9, 1942. Auschwitz. Yet another group of prisoners was stripped and marched into the gas chambers. Among them a Carmelite nun, Sister Teresa Benedicta of the Cross—Edith Stein.

Henry Bordeaux of the French Academy, writing a decade after her murder, wrote that she was, in effect, the symbol of all the victims of war and persecution in our century; but a willing victim, a model of those who offered their lives to atone for the crimes committed in a Christian nation gone mad.

Edith Stein was born at Breslau on October 12, 1891, the seventh child of a devout Jewish family. It was the Day of Atonement, a day of prayer and fasting, a day on which Jews have, over the long centuries, begged forgiveness for their sins.

The world into which she was born was comfortable and optimistic. It was Europe at the end of the nineteenth century—"the Age of Progress," which saw the invention of the steamboat, the locomotive, and the automobile. The work of Pasteur and Lister, among others, showed that many diseases could be controlled if not prevented, and portions of the world once hardly habitable now became areas of bustling human life.

The Age of Progress had also begun an era of colonial expansion. The major nations of Europe, as though by divine right, carved up the ancient lands of Africa and Asia, and grew rich from the natural resources found there.

It was, not without seeming justification, a time of almost easy optimism: progress was inevitable. Progress, of course, meant change, but every change was for the better. The growing belief that "God was simply Man writ large" became the religion of millions in Europe. But it was not the belief of Sigfrid and Auguste Stein. They were Jewish, and both proud of the fact and responsive to its demands.

Grace was said in Hebrew, and every ceremonial prescription of the Talmud was faithfully carried out. The walls bore large engravings illustrating scenes from the history of Israel, and the carvings on cupboards and chests depicted only motifs from the Old Testament. It might well have been, thought one visitor, the home of a rabbi.

But Sigfrid Stein was not a rabbi; he owned a lumber business, which was just beginning to expand when he died unexpectedly two years after Edith was born. Auguste Stein was left with seven children and an uncertain future.

She made a decision typical of her, but unusual for a widow in her time. She herself took over management of her husband's business, and although she knew nothing about timber, she soon learned. Her technical knowledge became such that she could glimpse a stand of timber from a train and calculate precisely the value of its wood.

The business prospered, but her children thought that due less to her hard work and acumen than to her goodness. She bought whole lots of timber so that the poor could have fuel in winter, and many a struggling carpenter or craftsman would buy wood from Frau Stein only to find his money returned.

Looking back on those years Edith Stein wrote: "It

was not a matter of education exactly. As children we read right conduct in our mother's example as if in a mirror of her virtues." Upon her children, growing up in a world increasingly secularized, this deeply faithful Jewess impressed that there was only one true standard of conduct, the law of God.

Next to her mother, the person who probably influenced the formation of Edith most was Else, the eldest child, upon whom fell much of the care of the other children and the running of the household. From Else we learn that Edith's childhood was far from joyless. As so often happens with the youngest, her brothers and sisters all but spoiled her, and passed on to her what they themselves were just learning at school.

The Stein home was, indeed, strict in its Jewish observances, but only a false piety thinks that God frowns when His children laugh. From Edith and her inseparable next-oldest sister Erna we get a picture of a loving, joyous family, and a childhood playmate recalled, years after, that "birthdays at the Steins' were a very special kind of festival."

Edith Stein's school days are remembered by her sister Erna and a classmate. They show a girl of a keen mind which was exceptionally gifted for the study of literature and language but which found mathematics and science difficult. The classmate who recalls those days had exactly the opposite qualities of mind. Fortunately she and Edith shared the same desk, and could prompt or copy from each other as the particular subject required. In a marvelous phrase, the schoolmate writes, "We formed a perfect team."

But the same schoolmate also writes that despite Edith's hard work and ambition to be first, she was always second, due less to her failings "than to a latent anti-Semitism from which our German schools were not free even then." It was then Hamlet's "cloud no bigger than a man's hand," which would in the ensuing years darken the whole of Europe and bring death to more than six million non-Aryans, including Edith Stein.

The phrase "non-Aryans" is significant. Hitler and the Nazis regarded Germans as the master race because they were Aryans. All others, particularly Slavs and Jews, were *Untermenschen*—subhumans.

The Nazis vowed to exterminate those of the Jewish race, not necessarily of the Jewish religion. Were that not the case, Edith Stein would not have been caught in the net they began to fling over Europe once Hitler came to power in 1933. For Edith Stein had abandoned the Jewish religion in her early youth. "I was," she wrote, "an atheist from my thirteenth to my twenty-first year."

When Frau Stein asked, Edith would accompany her to the synagogue, but the readings and rituals which seemed to sweep her mother beyond earth and time into an absorption with God no longer touched her daughter. Edith would neither speak nor act what she did not think to be true. But what was true? It was the search for truth, wherever the path might lead, that now dominated her, and the path led her into the lives of some of the most influential philosophers of our century. Foremost among them was Edmund Husserl.

Serious students (if their means permit) usually choose a university, not because of its prestige, but because of what they hope to learn from one or two professors in their chosen fields who happen to be teaching there. For Edith Stein, that professor was Edmund Husserl (*"the* philosopher of our age," she wrote) and the university was Goettingen in central Germany, scarcely numbered among the most prestigious of that period.

Husserl had begun a revolution in German philosophy by insisting that we live in a world objectively real which the human mind can know. If that seems like

common sense, it is. Husserl was a revolutionary precisely because he was a reactionary—reacting against
the school which had dominated German thought for
over a century—Kantian idealism, which taught that
whatever lies outside my mind cannot really be
grasped by my mind.

Part of Husserl's "reaction" was a return to Scholasticism, the philosophy which had Thomas Aquinas for
its greatest expositor. Husserl himself had learned
Scholasticism in Vienna, where, as a nonbelieving Jew,
he studied under two Catholic philosophers, one a former priest and the other a priest sometimes judged
unorthodox in his theology but always "orthodox" in
his philosophy.

Edith's ambition of studying under Husserl was realized more fully than she could have dared to dream.
"The Master," as his students called him, recognized
not only the brilliance of his new pupil, but her whole-
souled commitment to the goal of all philosophy. "The
pursuit of truth," she later wrote of herself, "was my
only passion."

But this passionate search for truth did not turn her
into a scholarly recluse, as it might have done. "She
had a genius for friendship," in the words of a contemporary—and some of the most charming pages of her
autobiographical writings tell of hiking trips with fellow students in the hills around Goettingen and ani-
mated philosophic discussions in cafés. In the circle
around Husserl, there was one for whom Edith developed a great affection, Adolph Reinach, a philosophy
tutor and Husserl's "right-hand man," as Edith termed
him. He had married six months before Edith came to
Goettingen, and he and his young wife immediately
took her into their affections. Neither the Reinachs nor
the young student could know then the role they were
to play in her life.

Another who influenced Edith was Max Scheler.

Like Husserl, he was a phenomenologist: unlike Husserl, he introduced specifically Catholic ideas into his lectures. "This was my first contact," she wrote, "with a world which had so far remained entirely unknown to me, and even though it did not lead me to the faith it did open up for me a whole region of 'phenomena' which I could no longer blindly pass by."

Her years at Goettingen were full, and she was happy. One can catch, in her words, the rapture she seemed to feel during this period of her life. "Dear old Goettingen! I don't believe that any one who did not study there between 1905 and 1914, during the short spring-time of the Goettingen phenomenology school, could ever imagine what that name conjures up for us."

Goettingen, Germany, and the world were to change in 1914. Those European powers which had carved up most of Asia and Africa among themselves had eyed each other nervously for more than a decade. By 1914 two rival alliances faced each other: the Triple Alliance of Germany, Austria-Hungary, and Italy, and the Triple Entente of England, France, and Russia.

The clash between the power blocs came, as Bismarck had predicted it would, over "some damn foolish thing in the Balkans"—the assassination in Sarajevo of Franz Ferdinand, heir to the Hapsburg throne of Austria. Two shots, fired by a nineteen-year-old boy, killed the archduke and his wife, and ignited a war which, before its end four years later, would involve thirty nations with a combined population of 1.4 billion people on six continents.

At Goettingen, as at more famous universities throughout Europe, both students and professors were mobilized, and the lecture halls became almost empty. Adolph Reinach volunteered for the Army shortly after Germany entered the war. In April 1915, Edith Stein joined the Red Cross as a nurse's aide.

She had dutifully written her mother, asking her

blessing; telling Frau Stein that the nursing assignment would be in Moravia at a hospital for Austrian soldiers sent back from the front with various contagious diseases. Her mother wrote back: "I forbid this. These soldiers are not only ill but are covered with lice. Edith, you will not go with my permission." Her daughter replied, "Then I shall have to go without it."

At the hospital as at the university she gave herself totally to her work, and was loved by the sick and wounded soldiers as she had been by her professors and fellow students.

She returned to Goettingen in September to resume her doctoral studies. By the following winter she had completed her dissertation and in August 1916 took her oral examinations, the very name of which, the *Rigorosum*, was calculated to strike fear into the candidate's heart. She passed the examination summa cum laude, and was now "Fraulein Doktor Edith Stein."

Husserl had been appointed that same year to a full professorship at the University of Freiburg. His assistant at Goettingen, Adolph Reinach, was still serving in the Army, and Husserl, moving now to a more prestigious university, invited Edith to be his assistant. Even the intellectually ambitious Edith Stein could scarcely have hoped for more: to be, at the age of twenty-five, the handpicked assistant of one of Europe's most famous philosophers, teaching courses to introduce students to "the Master's" phenomenological method and given the task of bringing order to the thousands of his shorthand notes and papers.

She was, however, to return to Goettingen once more to undertake a labor of love which she nonetheless dreaded. News came in November 1917 that Reinach had been killed in battle. Husserl asked Edith to represent him at the funeral, and Reinach's widow had requested her to put her slain husband's papers in order.

Edith's memories had been of a young, blissfully married Jewish couple, the wife ideally suited to a man whose brilliant future as professor of philosophy seemed assured. To face the widow now, bereaved and broken, filled Edith with anguish.

But the young widow, bereaved, was not broken. She and her husband had become Christians the year before his death. His wife now accepted his loss as her sharing in the sacrifice of the Cross, "which brings healing and life to all," as she told Edith. Death and Resurrection. "I accept in my heart," said Frau Reinach, "that Adolph now lives with God. He has reached his goal."

Edith said nothing at that time to the woman whose faith sustained and even sweetened her grief. But shortly before her own death thirty-five years later Edith Stein wrote of this experience: "It was then that I first encountered the Cross and the divine strength which it inspires in those who bear it. It was the moment in which my unbelief was shattered, Judaism paled, and Christ streamed out upon me: Christ in the mystery of the Cross."

The "phenomenon" of Christian faith became more evident as she reviewed Adolph Reinach's papers. As a philosopher he had been as passionately committed to the search for truth as she, but his writings revealed that he had taken other paths—some of which she never knew, and some of which she rejected.

One path was prayer, so much a part of her Jewish home and heritage. Reinach had come to look on prayer as a discovery of truth. "Through prayer," he wrote, "I am in touch with the ultimate background of the world." But the ultimate background of the world had become flesh and dwelt among us. "It is hard to say," wrote Reinach, "what one feels before the whole Christ: in Him God's Being, outside of time and be-

yond the world, seems to unfold itself in time and before the world."

From Max Scheler she had learned that one could be
a recognized philosopher and a Christian. But Adolph
Reinach had led her to a height which the young atheist found dizzying: a man she revered, whose mind she
admired, had come to believe that Christ was God, and
prayer a path to ultimate truth.

Edith Stein had much to ponder when she returned
to Freiburg to resume her duties as Husserl's assistant.
The "phenomenon of faith" had been shown to her, not
as an interesting possibility, but as the central reality in
the lives of two people to whom she was bound by the
ties of affection and esteem.

The First World War ended in 1918, the first war in
history wherein even the victors were vanquished. Germany had left dead on the battlefield twelve percent of
its men between the ages of fifteen and fifty, but
France and England had lost proportionately even
more. Portions of nations lay in utter ruins, and European civilization had almost to be built anew.

Edith Stein had immersed herself in both German
history and literature, and was proud of her German
heritage. Without abandoning philosophy, she now became actively involved in politics, hoping to contribute
to a new, chastened, and even greater Germany than
the one which was now suffering all the pangs of an
humiliating defeat.

She gave her energies to the German Democratic
Party, which tried to put postwar Germany in a middle
position between the still militant nationalism of the
Right and the extreme socialism of the Left. Ever the
philosopher, she also wrote an extended essay on the
nature and function of the State. Few women have
ever written substantial treatises on political theory,
and of these fewer still have written while still in their
twenties. Her study of politics is a measure of the un-

usual intelligence which was so much a part of Edith Stein.

One would have thought that if this still agnostic Jewish intellectual were to turn to Catholicism, it would have been through a process of reading theology. Her mind had already been opened to Christianity by thinkers such as Scheler and Reinach. What more natural, then, than to test that Christianity by reading its best expositors objectively, "without blinkers," as Husserl had constantly enjoined his students to approach any subject of inquiry.

But we have no evidence to suggest that Edith Stein chose this path, any more than she was responsible for Scheler's lecturing at Goettingen or had asked to represent Husserl at Reinach's funeral or put his papers in order.

The last stage of her journey toward faith was as seemingly adventitious as had been her meeting with the mind of Scheler and the Reinachs. Among Edith's many friends was Hedwig Conrad-Martius, herself a student of Husserl's at Freiburg. She and her husband owned a farm near Bergzabern, where they invited Edith to spend as much of her free time as she wished. During one of her visits, in the summer of 1921, both Hedwig and her husband were away for the evening. Edith went to the bookcase and picked out a volume almost at random. It was the autobiography of St. Teresa of Avila.

Her selection of a book to read before sleep may, at that time, have seemed random to Edith; but later in life she wrote that everything in our lives, down to the smallest detail, is arranged by the hands of God's providence. Among the books she might have chosen from the shelf was the *Confessions* of St. Augustine, one of the greatest books ever written. In telling his own story Augustine writes the biography of Everyman; the *Confessions* had deeply influenced Teresa of Avila. But

Edith Stein chose at "random" the work, not of the master, but of his student. "I began to read, was at once captivated, and did not stop until I finished. As I closed the book, I said, 'That is the truth.'"

She never detailed what burst upon her as the truth after reading Teresa's autobiography. But it is easy enough to surmise. Teresa, unlike Edith, had comparatively little formal education. But the two women, separated by centuries and totally different in temperament, shared a hunger for truth. Teresa had found this in God, Who is not only Truth "but the Love on which all other loves depend."

Edith finished the book at sunrise, and that morning went into the town to buy a Catholic catechism and a missal. These now became the subjects of her study, their simplicity in such contrast to the dense philosophical writings of Husserl and her own contributions which appeared in the *Yearbook for Philosophy and Phenomenological Research.*

On New Year's Day, 1922, the Feast of Christ's Circumcision, she was baptized in the Church of St. Martin at Bergzabern. She chose as her baptismal name Teresa, and her sponsor (years before most people could spell "ecumenism," let alone pronounce it) was her Protestant friend who had Teresa of Avila's *Life* in her bookcase, Dr. Hedwig Conrad-Martius. It is she who recalls that on this day, baptism followed by her First Communion, Edith had "the happiness of a child, and this was most beautiful."

But Edith was still her mother's child, and living once more at home. Frau Stein had been hurt when she knew that her daughter had lost her faith in the God of Abraham, Isaac, and Jacob, going to the synagogue not to praise Yahweh, but only to please her mother. Edith, who was later to go calmly to her death in a crematorium, could not yet tell her mother that she had become a Catholic.

It was months after that Edith could find the courage to tell Frau Stein that the daughter who had brought her pain by being an apostate and then an atheist, would now bring even greater pain by having become a Christian. Each revered the other. Edith could not evade her burden by either silence or a letter. She knelt before her mother, looked into that lined, beloved face, and said, "Mother, I am a Catholic."

She had feared expulsion from the family; she had prepared herself for her mother's wrath; but she had not steeled herself against her mother's tears. Neither she nor any of her family had ever seen their mother weep—at death of husband, after long days struggling to raise a family and yet conduct a business, even through the seemingly impossible days of the First World War. Yet Frau Stein wept, and Edith's tears were mingled with her mother's.

It may have been that Frau Stein's grief was deepened by the fact that her daughter had chosen to be, not a Lutheran, but a Roman Catholic. One biographer tellingly quotes a member of the family:

We were all dumbfounded by the news and did not know whether to be more astonished at Edith or at our mother's behaviour. Edith's step was incomprehensible to us all.

We knew Catholicism only as it was to be found in the lowest social class in our East-Schleswig home, and thought Catholicism merely consisted in grovelling on one's knees and kissing the priest's toe. We simply could not conceive how our Edith's lofty spirit could demean itself to this superstitious sect.

Within this "superstitious sect" Edith had found wisdom and peace. She wished to follow this newly opened path in what seemed to her its logical direction —the life of a contemplative nun. But she had learned from Teresa to have a spiritual counselor, and to take his counsel seriously.

Her first guide was Canon Schwind of the Cathedral at Speyer, where she had received Confirmation in February 1922. She should not consider entering a religious order, he told her, until she had become more familiar with daily life as a Catholic. It is interesting, however, that his principal objection to the convert's desire to be a nun was the crushing effect it would have upon her mother—an objection which Edith came to share, realizing that it would fill Frau Stein "with a bitterness for which I could not be responsible."

But Canon Schwind also recognized that Edith could neither remain at home nor return to university life at Freiburg. Once again that Providence in which Edith had now come to trust completely shaped her life. The Dominican sisters asked her to teach German at their college for girls at Speyer. Here her desire to be a nun was at least partially filled: she was given a room within the convent and her teaching duties allowed her to join the nuns in their daily cycle of religious devotions, and to spend long hours in prayer in the chapel.

Within this Dominican setting she also undertook the study of the great Dominican thinker, Thomas Aquinas, whose approach to philosophy at first baffled her because it was so unlike the method of the phenomenologists who had formed her mind.

At this time she also came to know the writings of Cardinal Newman. Canon Schwind had introduced her to Erich Przywara, a creative Jesuit theologian with an international reputation. He became, in effect, her theological Husserl, to whom she turned for direction in her efforts to learn the intellectual foundations of her still young Catholic faith.

It was Przywara who had suggested that she study Aquinas—not through manuals and commentaries, but by immersing herself in his voluminous and often formidable writings. Przywara was also planning to bring out a German edition of Newman's writings, and asked Edith to translate the *Letters and Journals,* which cover the period from 1801 to his conversion in 1845 from Anglicanism to Roman Catholicism.

That accomplished, he next asked her to translate Newman's *The Idea of a University,* and next urged her to undertake Aquinas' *Quaestiones Disputatae de Veritate,* of which there was no adequate German translation. Because Przywara had suggested that she translate and not merely read, Edith Stein, with her own brilliant but disciplined mind, was plunged into the intellectual currents of Catholicism as revealed in the writings of two men who were both saints and scholars.

From Newman, and more especially from Aquinas, she also learned that "it is possible to regard scholarly work as a service of God." She records that for a long period after her conversion she had thought that she must abandon everything that did not seem to lead her directly to Him. From the examples of Aquinas and Newman she had come to learn that "the more deeply a soul is drawn to God, the more it must go out into the world to carry the divine life into it."

Edith had tried to make the school at Speyer her Nazareth, but her life was hidden no longer. She was now being asked to lecture on Thomism, and, once more at the suggestion of Fr. Przywara, she began to write and speak on the role of women in national life. Before her conversion she had been a feminist, and now she brought to the subject not only her philosophical acumen but her knowledge of Scripture and theology as well.

She was of the school (which still has many distinguished adherents) that thought men and women possessed distinct qualities of mind and personality. It is interesting (if not ironic) that Fr. Przywara, in attempting to describe Edith herself, uses terms which almost refute her views on distinct qualities. Przywara writes of "the double nature of her spiritual being: large feminine receptivity and companionship coupled with severe masculine objectivity."

In dealing with the role of women in the Church, however, Edith Stein was well ahead of her time. She insisted that the whole complex of sex, including its psychology and pathology, should be part of Catholic education. Women, she also felt, were discriminated against in the Church, since canon law excludes women from all sacred offices, contrary to the practice of the early Church.

Her writings on women led to more invitations to lecture, and the clarity and quiet effectiveness of her presentation led to yet more lecture engagements before large audiences in Switzerland and Austria as well as in Germany itself.

She had been teaching at Speyer from 1923 to 1930. She was now forty, and one of the outstanding figures in German Catholic life. She still yearned, however, to be a nun. She spent each Holy Week at the Benedictine abbey at Beuron, where Abbot Walzer became both her friend and spiritual director. But, as had Canon Schwind, he thought her vocation lay in continued writing and lecturing. Indeed, he suggested, the girl's school at Speyer was too narrow an arena for her intellectual gifts, and he urged Edith to apply for a lectureship at the University of Freiburg. At almost the same time an opening seemed to appear at her native university of Breslau.

Neither appointment was given her, but it was probably because she was a woman, a Catholic, and a Jew. In 1932 she accepted a post at the German Institute for Educational Theory at Muenster. In 1933, on January 30, Hitler came to full power in Germany. Anti-Semitism was now written into law, and violence against the Jews was not merely condoned but encouraged.

While making a Holy Hour the words of Pascal kept coming to Edith's mind: "Jesus is in agony until the end of the world." She later wrote:

> I said to the Lord as the words kept repeating themselves in my mind that it was His Cross that was now laid on the Jewish people. Most of my people did not understand that, but those who did had to bear it willingly in the name of all the others. I wanted to do that, if only He would show me how. When the service came to an end I felt that my wish had been granted, but I did not know in what way my bearing of the Cross would happen.

One thing, however, was clear. She could not retain her teaching post at the Institute. As the storms of anti-Semitism lashed Germany, she feared, with good warrant, that her remaining there might endanger the whole school. She wrote to Abbot Walzer:

> For more than a decade I have wished to enter the Carmelites. Because I am a Jew I cannot now find work in Germany. Please, Abbot, does this not seem to be a sign from God that my work for the Church as a lecturer, teacher, and writer is ended, and that God is calling me to follow a different path. May I go now to Carmel?

Abbot Walzer gave his consent, she was accepted as a novice by the Carmelite cloister at Cologne, and was prepared to follow "a different path." But first she must tell her mother. If Frau Stein had been almost shattered by Edith's conversion, what would be her reaction to her daughter's decision to enter a life which even many Catholics find all but incomprehensible?

The only member of the family who understood was her sister Rosa, who herself wanted to become a Catholic but had heroically denied herself that desire until after her mother's death. Frau Stein herself reacted exactly as Edith had feared. She wept, she pleaded, she argued that Edith seemed to be completely deserting both her family and her people at the very time Jews were being systematically harassed and actual persecution seemed almost inevitable. "In those weeks," Edith wrote, "I often thought: which of us will break down, my mother or I? But both of us held out to the last day."

The last day at home was Edith's forty-second birthday, and, that year, the end of the Jewish Feast of Tabernacles. Frau Stein and Edith took a streetcar to the synagogue, but after the service Edith's eighty-four-year-old mother insisted that they walk home, a distance of almost three miles. Edith recounts the scene:

> But I had to consent, for I could see that she wanted very much to talk with me undisturbed.
> "It was a beautiful sermon, wasn't it?"
> "Yes."
> "Then it is possible for a Jew to be pious?"
> "Certainly—if one has not learnt anything more."
> Then came the despairing reply:
> "Why have you learnt more? I don't want to say anything against him. He may have been a very good man. But why did he make himself God?"

It was Edith's birthday. Her brothers, sisters, nieces, nephews, and friends gathered at Frau Stein's. But Edith's departure the next day to embrace a life which seemed an ultimate rejection of Judaism cast a pall over the party. Frau Stein was, of course, the most sad and least comprehending. Edith wrote:

In the end my mother and I were alone in the room; my sisters were still clearing away and washing up. Then she hid her face in her hands and began to weep. I stood behind her chair and laid her silvery grey head on my breast. We stayed so for a long while, until she let me persuade her to go to bed. I took her upstairs and helped her to undress, for the first time in my life. Then I stayed sitting on her bed until she herself sent me to get some sleep. I think neither of us had any rest that night.

On October 13, 1933, her prayer over twelve years was answered. She entered the Carmel in Cologne. For Edith, in the words of her prioress, "it was a descent from the summit of a great career into the depths of insignificance." She was treated like any other postulant, and most of the nuns had never heard of her, although they must have wondered what this forty-two-year-old woman had been doing all her life. She could not sew, was a menace in the kitchen, and was clumsy and unskilled at any form of housework. For Fraulein Doktor Stein it was a school of humility, but she went through it with humor and good grace.

Many people, upon hearing that a woman has entered the Carmelites, think, "Oh, the poor dear has gone to her grave." From the prioress of Carmel we get the picture of a rather "lively graveyard":

Edith Stein was at home in the conventual family from the beginning. She used to laugh and joke like a child with the other sisters till the tears ran down her cheeks. She used to declare that she had never laughed so much in all her life as during recreation at Carmel. Everyone was at their ease with her.

On April 15, 1934, Edith was clothed in the Carmelite habit. Attending the ceremony were Abbot

Walzer, her friend and spiritual director from Beuron; her godmother, Dr. Conrad-Martius, at whose home she had read St. Teresa's life; a host of professors, former students, and friends. Missing were Edmund Husserl, who was ill, and Edith's family.

She chose the name Teresa Benedicta of the Cross: "Teresa" for the woman who had first led her to faith; "Benedicta" in gratitude for what she had learned of the Church's liturgical prayer at the Benedictine abbey at Beuron; "of the Cross" to express her devotion to the Crucified and her desire to share in His Passion.

When she had entered Carmel Edith Stein neither knew nor cared whether she would be allowed to continue her study and writing. Fortunately for her own and subsequent generations, her provincial asked her to keep on with her work. She was to be dispensed from all other duties (no more housework!) except spiritual ones.

She resumed the writing of *Potency and Act*, another effort to study St. Thomas and the phenomenologists in the light each threw upon the other. It took four years to complete this work of five hundred pages, and when completed it could not be published because the author was a non-Aryan.

Nor had the schoolteacher and lecturer died in Edith Stein. As Sister Benedicta she wrote on topics such as "The Mystery of Christmas" and "The Prayer of the Church" which for clarity of style and mastery of thought rank among the finest spiritual writings of our century.

She also wrote articles for more popular Catholic magazines, but here too the shadow of the future began to fall upon the present. She had already had several articles published in the magazine *Christian Woman*, but the last article she wrote was accepted but never published. It was becoming dangerous, even in

1935, for a Catholic journal to publish a Catholic but non-Aryan author.

Outside of the Carmel in Cologne Sister Benedicta's beloved Germany was being torn asunder. Jews had been deprived of citizenship; they were, officially, not citizens but "subjects." They were barred from the professions, the civil service, radio and journalism, teaching, and even farming. In many places Jews could not even buy necessities: a sign, "Jews Not Admitted," hung over food shops, and pharmacies would not sell them medicines.

The madness reached into every phase of German life. The universities now taught *German* physics, *German* chemistry, *German* mathematics, based on the monstrous myth of "racial sciences," extolling Germans as the only true scientists, and Jewish scientists as incapable of objectivity or of even telling the truth. Tragically, the number of professors in any field to oppose National Socialism was very small, and the universities became repositories of delusions and falsehood. To Sister Benedicta, with her passion for truth, her memories of three universities, and the translation of Newman, this degradation must have been almost as painful as the mounting persecution of the Jews.

There were, however, some consolations. Frau Stein had refused for years to answer any of the letters Sister Benedicta wrote from Carmel. But in the autumn of 1936 Frau Stein added her best wishes to one of the letters from Edith's older sister, Rosa. She continued to write a brief note in each of Rosa's letters; eventually, she even addressed Edith as "Sister Teresa." She probably did not understand her daughter's vocation any more clearly than she had at their parting, but at last she had come to accept it, and Edith was overjoyed.

She joyed, too, in Rosa, but the joy was bittersweet. Rosa still wished to become a Catholic, but both she and Edith continued to feel that she should not take

that step until after her mother's death. That came after
a year of illness, on September 14, 1936. It was the
Feast of the Exaltation of the Holy Cross, on which
Carmelites renew their vows. "When my turn came,"
Sister Benedicta told another nun after the ceremony,
"my mother was with me. I distinctly felt her presence." Later that day a telegram came from Breslau,
announcing Frau Stein's death. It had occurred at the
very hour when her daughter had renewed her vows.

At least Frau Stein, whose long life had centered on
her Jewish faith, was spared witnessing the full horror
of the Nazi persecution of her people, who were now
being hunted down and sent by the hundreds of thousands to labor camps or extermination.

During the nights of November 9 and 10, 1938,
mobs of Nazis roared through the streets of Germany,
burning or pillaging Jewish homes, shops, and even
synagogues. "This is the shadow of the Cross falling
upon my people," wrote Sister Benedicta. "But woe to
this city and this country when God shall avenge what
is today done to the Jews."

It now became clear to Sister Benedicta that her
very presence might bring Nazi reprisals against the
whole Carmelite convent in Cologne. Arrangements
were made for her to transfer to another Carmel at
Echt in Holland. On New Year's Eve 1938, the grief-
stricken nuns bade farewell to Sister Benedicta as she
left the house which had become for her the dearest
place on earth.

The shadow of the Cross now fell across the whole
of Europe. On September 1, 1939, Hitler invaded
Poland and triggered World War II. As country after
country fell before the German blitzkrieg the Jews in
the conquered nations met, by the millions, the fate
that had befallen most of the Jews in Germany.

But neither were Christians to be spared unless they
"worshiped the Beast." In 1935 Hitler had appointed a

friend, Hans Kerrl, as Minister for Church Affairs. Kerrl stated that "Christianity is not dependent upon the Apostle's Creed. True Christianity is represented by the [National Socialist] Party. The Fuehrer is the herald of a new revelation."

During the next years thousands of pastors, priests, nuns, and lay people were arrested, many on false charges of "immorality" or "smuggling foreign currency." In March 1937, Pope Pius XI had issued an encyclical charging the Nazi government of "secret and open fundamental hostility to Christ and His Church."

Sister Benedicta, however, seemed safe in the cloister at Echt, and her convent life was enriched when her sister Rosa was able to join her in the summer of 1940. After Frau Stein's death Rosa had been able to fulfill her long desire to become a Catholic, and now lived in the convent but outside the enclosure. Like Edith, Rosa had both the gift of prayer and a genius for friendship.

But the safety of Echt was short-lived. The Germans had swept over Holland and by the end of 1940 it lay completely under Hitler's heel. The persecution of the Jews and the harassment of resistant Christians began to assume the same pattern it had in Germany, Poland, and Czechoslovakia. The Carmelites began to fear for the Stein sisters and undertook negotiations to move them to a Swiss convent, an effort eventually blocked by Swiss officials.

Through this period of uncertainty, Sister Benedicta continued her study of the great Carmelite mystic, St. John of the Cross, who, with Teresa of Avila, is also a Doctor of the Church. Sister Benedicta called her work *The Science of the Cross*. It is a remarkable mingling of phenomenology and mysticism, and reveals, far beyond the author's intention, the heights to which her own soul had scaled. She was working on the final pages when the Gestapo arrested her and Rosa on August 2, 1942.

On that day every non-Aryan priest and religious was arrested and herded away. It was an act of reprisal against the Dutch bishops, who had written a strong pastoral letter condemning the Nazi treatment of the Jews.

The prisoners were taken to Westerbork in Holland, an assembly point where Nazi victims awaited transportation east to labor camps or death. On August 7, Sister Benedicta, Rosa, and some 1,200 other Catholic Jews were herded into the trains that would carry them to Auschwitz. There, on August 9, they were stripped and sent into the gas chambers. Edith Stein, whose life had been a passionate search for truth, now possessed It, and was possessed by It. Before leaving Westerbork she had managed to write a note which reached the Superior at Echt. "One can only learn the *Science of the Cross* if one feels the Cross in one's own person. I was convinced of this from the very first and have said with all my heart, 'Hail the Cross, our only hope.'"

In the years which have passed since Henry Bordeaux wrote of her, Edith Stein has emerged even more clearly as the symbol of all the victims of war and persecution in our time. But Edith Stein was not merely a victim; she was a martyr for, as Evelyn Underhill points out, "Love, after all, makes the whole difference between an execution and a martyrdom."

There have been many thousands of martyrs since— in the Gulags of Russia and Eastern Europe, in China, the Koreas and Philippines, in Latin America.

Some of these martyrs are known—Archbishop Romero, Ita Ford, Maura Clark, Dorothy Kazel, Jean Donovan slain in El Salvador in 1980—one land among many where to be a Christian is a crime.

But most martyrs in our increasingly violent century

are nameless. It is of these particularly that Edith Stein is symbol and speaker because she expressed so well their faith: "If we accept the whole Christ in faithful self-giving, He will lead us through His Passion and Cross to the glory of the Resurrection. After the Dark Night, the Living Flame of Love shines forth."

# PIERRE TEILHARD DE CHARDIN

*John Deedy*

They were two seemingly insignificant incidents in the process of growing up, but they raised large questions in a serious, astute, inquiring mind, and ultimately they helped cast the person in the mold that was to be his for life. He was Pierre Teilhard de Chardin, priest, paleontologist, philosopher.

The first of the incidents occurred when he was five and his mother was cutting his hair by the fireplace. A lock drifted into the flames, singed, curled, burned, turned to ash. The effect was unnerving. "An awful feeling came on me at that moment," Teilhard would one day reflect. "For the first time in my life I *knew* that I was perishable." The experience propelled him on a lifelong search for answers to life in a milieu where everything seemed evanescent and perishable, so easily turned to ashes and dust.

The second incident involved the world in which he first went looking for answers, his world of "idols," the plough spanner in the courtyard, the shell splinters from a nearby firing range, the rock fragments chipped from some mass of stone. A piece of iron seized his fascination, quickening his feeling for matter, his sense of the durable. He devised in his mind's eye a "God of Iron." Why iron? Because by his young perception "there was nothing in the world harder, tougher, more durable than this wonderful substance." Alas the disap-

pointment, the "child's despair," when he discovered
that iron could be scratched and that it could rust. "I
had to look elsewhere for substitutes that would con-
sole me," he remarked.

Eventually he found his satisfying answer in a God
of evolution, a God stirring in matter. His was a God
that led him as scientist across the face of much of the
earth in a study of geological periods and the development of humankind. Everywhere he saw God's energy
at work and a design that evolved toward fulfillment
through Christ the son. He would rhapsodize his belief,
turn it to prayer in his *Mass Upon the Altar of the
World:*

"Christ of glory, hidden power stirring in the heart
of matter, glowing center in which the unnumbered
strands of the manifold are knit together; strength inex-
orable as the world and warm as life; you whose brow
is of snow, whose eyes are of fire, whose feet are more
dazzling than gold poured from the furnace; you whose
hands hold captive the stars; you, the first and the last,
the living, the dead, the re-born; you, who gather up in
your superabundant oneness every delight, every taste,
every energy, every phase of existence, to you my
being cries out with a longing as vast as the universe:
for you indeed are my Lord and My God."

There was peace of soul, but also disillusionment.
For in discovering his God of evolution, Teilhard at the
same time encountered headache and heartache. The
God of his discovery was not the God of his Church.
Teilhard de Chardin served his Church for forty-three
years as a loyal Jesuit and a searching pilgrim. But his
search was much too revolutionary, his conclusions
much too unorthodox, certainly by standards of the
day. The scientific community revered him, but his
Church kept him at arm's length. Unappreciated by his
Church in his lifetime, Teilhard de Chardin is still not
fully appreciated in death. Nevertheless, as scientific

philosopher and mystic his life's story shows tracings of the very elements that go into the making of saints.

The broad strokes of Teilhard's life are familiar enough. This man of two worlds, the world of science and the world of religion, was born in Sarcenat in France on May 1, 1881, into a family that could claim lineage to Pascal on the paternal side and to Voltaire on the maternal. The Teilhard family was one of the oldest in the Auvergne, its roots reaching back to a fourteenth-century notary, another Pierre Teilhard. (The "de Chardin" is an appendage, of course, that arrived to the family name via a nineteenth-century marriage.) The latterday Pierre was the fourth of eleven children. He studied with the Jesuits beginning at the age of ten, and by all accounts distinguished himself as a student, except in the area of religious instruction. In mind and temperament he is said to have reacted not against what was taught, but the way in which it was taught. Even then his mind was reaching out for new, more satisfactory explanations for old truths and older facts of life and faith.

He entered the Jesuit order at Aix-en-Provence at age eighteen, did his teaching internship at the Jesuits' Holy Family College in Cairo, then went to England for theological studies. He was ordained a priest in 1912 by the Bishop of Southwark, Monsignor Amigo. Père Teilhard served in World War I, but not as a chaplain. He signed up as a stretcher bearer and was assigned to the 8th Regiment of Moroccan Tirailleurs, later to become the 4th Combined Tirailleurs and Zouaves. His bravery was exceptional; though but a corporal, he was awarded the Medaille Militaire and the Legion d'Honneur. His life was so charmed that the North African soldiers believed him to be miraculously protected by his *baraka*, his spiritual stature. French officers, on the other hand, thought him rash.

When one spoke to him of the odds he was daring, Teilhard replied with words that plumbed the depths of spirituality and belief: "If I'm killed, I will have changed my state, that's all."

Following the war, Teilhard taught at the Institut Catholique in Paris, at the same time earning a doctorate in paleontology from the Sorbonne in 1922. From 1923 to 1946, he was in China and the Far East, there making a remarkable name for himself both as paleontologist and geologist. He was involved in the discovery of Peking Man and made a number of other finds that vastly enlarged scientific knowledge about the dates of Asia's fossils, its sedimentary deposits and its stratigraphical correlations. His research nourished theological theories about evolution, and these Teilhard set down in his master work, *The Phenomenon of Man*. The book was to be both cross and crown. It never appeared in his lifetime. When the manuscript was submitted to Rome for permission to publish, it only served to confirm doubts deriving from Teilhard's privately circulated writings—what he called his *clandestins;* what Rome ominously referred to as his "more or less secret and mysterious" tracts. The conclusion was that this was a dangerous, perhaps heretical thinker. Teilhard, crushed but dutiful, submitted to Rome's decision that *The Phenomenon of Man* "pass[ed] beyond the bounds of 'science' properly defined." But never for a minute did he believe himself wrong. And least of all did he regard himself as heretical.

For Rome, Teilhard's "heresy" was not only in embracing evolution—Rome being then firmly wedded to Genesis—but in presenting it as a continuing Christological process. By Teilhard's reasoning, man (in the manner of the times, his generic term for humankind) was not a static center of the world. Rather, man was the axis, the very "arrow" of evolution. Evolution, in turn, was an irreversible process planned by God and converging ultimately on God, as the universe continued to perfect itself through the evolving intelligence of man.

Teilhard posited a starting point (Alpha) and a goal (the Omega Point). Each in effect is God, so that what began in God returns in time to God.

The concept was so novel as to require a new vocabulary. Thus, cosmogenesis became Teilhard's word to indicate the development of a world in which man is central. Hominization described the progressive movement of nonreflective animal life toward reflective human life. Noögenesis identified the growth of man's mind, and noösphere signified the new layer of evolution beyond others scientifically classified. Noösphere is not, however, the apex of evolution. Man moves on, the mind taking over where instinct has left off. Accordingly, man does not have to develop wings biologically in order to fly. The noösphere has occurred, hence the airplane. Further, as the universe becomes increasingly hominized, man converges inexorably on the superior pole, the Omega Point, the Risen Christ, God.

Teilhard was as sure of his propositions as of tomorrow's dawn. For the Christian, he maintained, the final biological success of man on earth is not a simple probability, but a certitude. "Without biological evolution which produced the brain, there would be no sanctified souls," he held. "Similarly, without the evolution of collective thought, which alone can realize on earth the fullness of human consciousness, could there be a consummated Christ? In other words, without the constant striving of every human cell to unite with all the others, would the Parousia be physically possible?" Certitude rested in the fact that "Christ (and in Him, virtually, the world) is already Risen."

Rome frowned. Teilhard was a pantheist. His concepts were much too exotic. A God of evolution, a Christ of cosmogenesis! They did not leave room for special creation, for divine grace. Where, it was asked, is the Fall in Teilhard's picture? Where is Grace? Where is Redemption? Where is the place of God himself within the evolutionary cycle?

The answers were not always ready, or satisfactory. Sometimes the questions were not even addressed. It was not that Teilhard was contemptuous of them. It was rather that he did not regard their answering as being within his responsibility. He was a scientist, not a theologian. Or, as one biographer remarked, his was the task to lead people "to the porch of the temple." Others should take over from there.

There was no persuasion for Rome in any of this. Rome was grateful, no doubt, for Teilhard's loyalty; it was relieved by his willingness to seek permission before publishing, and it welcomed his compliance with hard decisions. But it could do without his theories on the "power and the worth of the Christian potential" struggling for release in a world of continuing evolution. Rome elected to contain Teilhard—and in the process it shaped a man of heroic virtue, whose patience and endurance, spiritual and emotional, exceeded the capacities of most mortals.

Teilhard was a gentle man, and even his enemies found it difficult to be bluntly cruel to the man. Accordingly, there was nothing so extreme as excommunication. But there was systematic repression, and it was this that forged the character of the man.

To begin with, there was censorship. There was the denial of teaching positions. There was the snubbing of his professional credentials when time came to name Church representatives to learned scientific conferences. There was *Humani Generis*, Pius XII's encyclical of August 12, 1950, warning against attempts to distort Catholic truths. *Humani Generis* did not cite Teilhard by name, but it may as well have. It was aimed, in

Teilhard's viewpoint, at all who "sought to enrich our understanding of the grandeur of Christ."

Finally, there were those nudges into "exile," Teilhard's superiors all the way to Rome obviously preferring for him to be somewhere, anywhere where he would be less likely to add to theological ferments. New York City, a theological wasteland in the 1950s, was such an outposting, and it was there between November 26, 1951, and April 10, 1955, that the last lines were written to Teilhard's long tale of humiliation.

The "containment" exacted its toll on Teilhard's well-being, and his psyche. There were bitter tears, frequent bouts of depression, and obsessive worries that in obeying orders he was doing violence to truth and conscience. Driven to the emotional wall, Teilhard gave thought to leaving the Jesuits for the secular priesthood, where he might be freer to publish and to promote ideas on which he was convinced the effective future of the Church depended. But he stayed a Jesuit, concluding after much soul-searching and prayer that to quit the order would be to deny his vocation and undercut the spirit of Christian community, which he felt was part of his evolutionary message to commend. It was a difficult decision and Teilhard poured out his anguish to a fellow Jesuit:

"If I rebelled (humanly, it would be so easy and so sweet), I would betray my belief that Our Lord activates all events. Moreover, I would compromise the religious value of my ideas in the eyes of our own brothers, if not others. They would see an estrangement from the Church, pride, who knows what. It is essential I show, by my example, that if my ideas are novel, they make me no less faithful. But there are shadows. Which of my two vocations is more sacred—the one I followed in my boyhood, at eighteen, or the one revealed to me in the fullness of my manhood as the true meaning? Oh, my friend, tell me that by obeying I am not being false to my ideals."

It was not the first time that Teilhard's spirits bordered on despair, nor would it be the last. He prayed, and he asked his friends to pray, for strength to persevere. Especially he prayed that he would not die embittered. Many of the prayers were directed to the Sacred Heart of Jesus, for as much as it may surprise some sophisticated Catholics, devotion to the Sacred Heart figured prominently in Teilhard's spirituality.

Devotion to the Sacred Heart came to Teilhard through his "dear and sainted" mother, a woman of almost storybook piety and so trusting in God that when a priest sought to comfort her on the death of one of her children, she remarked, "No, why trouble? He is in heaven before us." There was a plaque over the main entrance of the Teilhard house dedicating it to the Sacred Heart, and early on, Teilhard would tell us, devotion to the Sacred Heart lit up his infant soul. Teilhard was disapproving of certain forms that popular devotion to the Sacred Heart took. Yet into his last years he stayed attached to the Sacred Heart. The embracing of the Sacred Heart, he said, with all the symbolism it expresses, enabled him "to escape from all that pained him so deeply in the organization of the body of Christ," the institutional Church.

To the bumpy end, Teilhard remained "a child of obedience." But the child of obedience had become over the years a veteran of many skirmishes. This seasoned Teilhard had his posthumous triumph, for not only did *The Phenomenon of Man* see the light of day, but so did scores of manuscripts more. (The card file on Teilhard is inches thick in the major libraries of the world.) In 1957, seeking to head off Teilhardism, Rome banned Teilhard's writings from Catholic bookstores. Five years later, in 1962, it issued a *monitum*, or formal warning, against uncritical acceptance of the ideas

of Teilhardism. But Teilhardism was loose in the world.
The victim had outlived the victimizers—or, more
specifically, had outmaneuvered them. And therein lies
a problem, though not an insurmountable one, for ad-
mirers of all that Teilhard stood for as a Catholic. He
foiled Rome by an uncharacteristic act of independence.

Rome was foiled by a small scrap of paper. Teilhard
made a will providing for the disposition of his manuscripts. Under pressure from associates, he sat down
one day and scratched out a note naming an acquaintance, Mlle. Jeanne Mortier, as legatee of his papers.
There was no battery of lawyers around, no news cam-
era—just Teilhard, Mlle. Mortier, Father Raymond
Jouve, friend and acting superior at *Études*, the Jesuit
periodical house (it was July and the regular superior
was away), and the porter, Brother Cochet. It was a
modest setting for an act that was historic and, under
the circumstance, not exactly humble: Teilhard's drawing up of a will. Teilhard was uncomfortable, brusque.
He wrote the words of consignment, and as the hand
moved the lips asked, "And in the case that you are in-
disposed, who else?" Mlle. Mortier, somewhat awe-
struck: "Jean Piveteau, André George, François Ri-
chaud . . . ?" He put the names down, discussed no
details, handed her the paper, and was done with it.
He did not savor the moment.

That scrap of paper is ammunition for devil's advo-
cates, as Jesuits are not supposed to make wills. As
members of the Society of Jesus, they surrender material possessions to it. What they own is the society's. In
making a will, Teilhard appeared to contravene that
tradition and be in violation at least of his vow of poverty.

In making a will, Teilhard acted with great reluctance. He took his vows seriously, and he was not anx-
ious to convey even a semblance of disloyalty to the

order. He wanted to depart the society in death as he had entered it as a youth, in good standing and with total dignity. On the other hand, there was the work of a lifetime to insure, if not for his own intellectual satisfaction, then for the good of the Church he loved unqualifiedly. For what was involved was a body of work which he considered essential to the Church's mission to "amorize" and "valorize" the world—to teach it to love, to teach it to know its own worth. That work had to be protected. Teilhard was the most unjesuitical of Jesuits, but he would accept the judgment of a canon lawyer who happened to be visiting at Études. Teilhard did not consult directly with the canonist. Jouve seized the initiative, presenting Teilhard's case to him in purely hypothetical context. He was told that ecclesiastical law was ambiguous on whether the vow of poverty extended to one's papers and manuscripts. Relayed to Teilhard, the judgment was enough to seed moral doubt and leave Teilhard free to choose the more favorable option. Accordingly, Teilhard could make a will with a certain ease of conscience. If the spirit of the vow was broken, the letter was not.

(The vow of obedience seems also to have been impinged upon by Teilhard's decision, but this vow appears not to have been a focus of great concern to Teilhard's advisers, perhaps because it was deemed that its primary applications lay elsewhere, or perhaps because its applications in this case were so obviously superseded by considerations of the greater good—the preservation of a body of work taking precedence over observance of a minor rule of conduct.)

If there is an embarrassing detail in any brief that ever makes its way to the arbiters of canonization, it is this matter of the will. Still, it is a difficulty that one would expect to overcome itself. For if there had been no will, there would by that time have been no remembering Teilhard, either his thought or his attributes. He would long since have faded into the footnotes of history, a person with some interesting theories, most of them unpublished, many of them lost or destroyed, and therefore all of them too fragmentary to commend the man to posterity—and with the man, the example of his life.

Teilhard's Catholicism, needless to say, was as cerebral as it was controversial. The discovering of God in "the Christ universal," the pursuit of a "new God of evolution" who is simultaneously personal and "ultra-humanizing"—nothing of this is intellectually or devotionally easy, then or now. It is not your orthodox, everyday notion of what Catholicism is all about. The paradox is that, despite its esoteric strains, Teilhard's Catholicism had its formal side, and with aspects of this—notably devotion to the Blessed Virgin and commitment to the Mass—no one in the pews, front or back, would have much trouble identifying. Indeed, as devotion to the Sacred Heart helped Teilhard cope with the trials of institutional Catholicism, Mary and the Mass helped nourish soul and spirit.

Teilhard's devotion to Mary was "tender and loving," and she occupied a prominent place in his ideation of generative evolution. There was also the important pragmatic consideration that devotion to Our Lady brought a necessary corrective balance to a Christianity otherwise heavily weighted in the masculine. Thus, when the dogma of the Assumption was formally defined in 1950, Teilhard would worry about the provocation that the declaration presented to physics and biology because of the "limited language and resources of present theological thinking." At the same time, however, he would welcome the declaration, because he saw the "biopsychological necessity" of the Marial "compensating for the masculinity of Jahweh in our piety." In this context, his becomes one of the early recognitions of the sexist imbalances of traditional Catholicism.

To Teilhard, Mary as woman and mother was "the incorruptible beauty of the times to come." She was to be esteemed and loved, and devotion to her, including the rosary, was to be encouraged. As with devotion to the Sacred Heart, Teilhard regarded the rosary as being vulnerable to devotional excesses. Nonetheless, the rosary appealed to him as a devotion that could be transformed into a prayer of sympathy, the heart of Mary becoming a kind of mirror in which the whole structure of dogma was reflected. In the process, the rosary's sequence of mysteries, joyful, sorrowful and glorious, became a mirroring of the human condition and thus a further aid to prayer.

But above all else, it was the Mass that was central to Teilhard's spirituality and that provided psychological as well as religious comfort. Being central to his spirituality, the Mass also became linked to Teilhard's scientific philosophy. The Mass in Teilhard's view was the channel by which the Risen Christ was perpetually renewed in the world and thus was a vital energizing element in the ultimate convergence of the world on the God of evolution. In this context, the Mass was the extension of the Incarnation of the Word, the promise of the world's transfiguration.

The supreme moment, of course, was the consecration. For Teilhard, the words *This is My Body. . . . This is My Blood* sped beyond the altar, beyond the congregation. They extended out to the cosmos itself and nourished the entire mystical body. In a sense, the substance of the Eucharist became a reflection of the world's development during that day, "the bread symbolizing appropriately what creation succeeds in producing, the wine (the blood) what creation causes to be lost in exhaustion and suffering in the course of its effort."

In Teilhard's mind, the Mass and the Eucharist were tied to the evolutionary process itself: "As our humanity assimilates the material world, and as the host assimilates our humanity, the Eucharistic transformation goes beyond and completes the transubstantiation of the bread on the altar. Step by step it irresistibly invades the universe. It is the fire that sweeps over the hearth, the stroke that vibrates through the bronze. In a secondary and generalized sense, but in a true sense, the sacramental species are formed by the totality of the world, and the duration of creation is the time needed for its consecration."

In his quest for holiness and in his conviction that he as priest was part of God's evolutive plan, Teilhard was conscientious about celebrating daily Mass, and helping others celebrate Mass. When he was living in a religious community, as for a time in New York City, he followed the practice of the priest who had just said Mass serving the Mass of the next priest to the altar. This was the period, of course, when private Mass was common and when one could visit certain churches and find Masses being celebrated seriatim in chapels and at side altars. Teilhard's Mass was simple, devout, correct—which is to say rubrical in the precise pre-Vatican Council II manner. It was nothing to be said hurriedly or carelessly. The wife of the Vichy ambassador to Japan, Mme. Yolande Arsène-Henri, once commented, "Whoever has not seen Teilhard say Mass has seen nothing."

The Mass mattered, and without the bread and wine with which to offer Mass, as happened at times on expeditions into remote areas, Teilhard was a man deprived, indeed sometimes a man in spiritual anguish. On one such occasion—of an Easter Sunday in the Ordos Desert of Inner Mongolia—he composed the prayer that laid bare the soul and stands as a testament of faith:

"Since once again, O Lord, in the steppes of Asia, I have no bread, no wine, no altar, I will raise myself above those symbols to the pure majesty of Reality, and I will offer to You, I, Your priest, upon the altar of the entire earth, the labor and the suffering of the world. . . .

"Receive, O Lord, in its totality the Host which Creation, drawn by Your magnetism, presents to You at the dawn of a new day. This bread, our effort, is in itself, I know, nothing but an immense disintegration. This wine, our anguish, as yet, alas! is only an evaporating beverage. But in the depths of this inchoate mass You have placed—I am certain, for I feel it—an irresistible and holy desire that moves us all, the impious as well as the faithful, to cry out: 'O Lord, make us one!'"

Prayer was a constant in his life.

On another day, unable to celebrate Mass because of an accident that had temporarily disabled him, Teilhard asked George Barbour, the American geologist, to read sections of the Breviary to him in bed.

For all his love for the Mass and his belief in the centrality of the Mass in the divine plan, Teilhard was not a spectacular homilist. He could appreciate a good sermon, and therefore he could admire the gifts of a Monsignor Fulton J. Sheen—his diction, his delivery, his feeling (although Teilhard wondered at Sheen's ability "to see and live a religion without Mysteries," apart from those of theology). But the homily was just not Teilhard's forte. Even so, a remarkable sermon survives which speaks both of Teilhard's spirituality and his ability to reach out and touch people of all persuasions. It is a sermon delivered before Mass on New Year's Day of 1932, in a little chapel "lost" in the heart of China, the congregation being the team that comprised a Citroën-sponsored expedition across Turkestan and Mongolia. Teilhard was the official geologist on the expedition, and no one in the group other than himself was a practicing Catholic. Yet Teilhard had the power to bring the entire party together before a common God for Mass and for this homily:

"My dear friends. Here we are this morning, all together in this little church . . . to begin this new year in the face of God. God, no doubt, has not the same precise meaning, the same face, for each of us. But because we are all men, none of us can escape the sense . . . that above us and in front of us there exists a higher energy, in which we must recognize—since it is higher—the enlarged equivalent of our own intelligence and will. It is in this powerful Presence that we should be recollected for a moment at the beginning of this year. We ask this Presence to unite us . . . with those whom we love, far away. . . . And we beg His all-powerful Presence . . . to crown our enterprise with success, and that any suffering which may befall us . . . may be transformed in the higher joy of taking our little place in the universe and having done what was our duty. It is so that this may happen that I shall offer to Him, for all of you, this Mass—the highest form of Christian prayer."

Perhaps Teilhard was not an especially noted homilist because deep down he was not a moralizer. People who approached him with moral or spiritual problems received advice that generally was much too indirect and certainly far too rarefied for any pulpit. Helmut de Terra, the German geologist, once confided his doubts and anxieties to Teilhard when they were together in Philadelphia. Teilhard's response, in de Terra's words, was essentially an appeal to de Terra's own ability "to find the right road." "He seemed content to profess his fatih in me," said de Terra, "to place his entire reliance on mental energy as the essence of spirituality." One can see where such a person would have trouble mastering a pulpit.

For those who could communicate on Teilhard's intellectual level, however, the results of a spiritual conference could be marvelously satisfying. One such was Max de Bégouën, son of the French speleologist Comte de Bégouën and a close friend. He confided in Teilhard one night in Paris. It was after a dinner party, shortly after the Armistice of 1918. Bégouën has recorded the night: "It was raining and cold. As I walked beside him, I told him I had lost my faith and why. Very simply, with the kindness and charity that never failed him, he expounded his ideas on evolution, and the supreme and active part Christ played in the evolution of the cosmos. From nine to midnight, walking back and forth in the rain, Father Teilhard . . . gave me the answer I had waited for so long. That night I was born to life—staggering like Lazarus as he came out of the tomb when the Lord called to him: 'Come forth!'"

Teilhard's faith was so cerebral that at times it troubled even himself. Thus, after the death of his sister Marguerite—sweet "Guiguite" who directed the Catholic Union of the Sick from a sickbed to which she was confined for seventeen years by tuberculosis of the spine—Teilhard would anxiously contrast his mission of faith to hers:

"O Marguerite, my sister, while I was rushing across land and sea, dedicated to the positive forces of the universe, passionately concerned with the sight of all the colors of the earth, you were lying immobile; silently, and in the secret depths of your being, changing the darkest shadows of the world into light. Tell me, in the eyes of the Creator, which of the two of us had the better part?"

This was Teilhard examining his conscience, wondering on paper whether his intellectual gifts were playing tricks with reason and balance. He had cause to wonder, for not only had his intellect placed him on a level above most of his contemporaries, it also seems to have placed him apart from issues and concerns one would expect to engage the interests of a priest, certainly one as sensitive as himself. Teilhard, for instance, was curiously detached from social and human problems, and great tragedies, such as World War II, failed to wring his soul. It was almost as if tragedies large or small were an inevitable part of the working out of the evolutionary process. Even in small human details he could be a man apart. For example, despite all his years in China, he never got close enough to the Chinese as a people to learn their language with any expertise.

On the other hand, Teilhard was capable of large human kindnesses. De Terra tells of returning after a hard day's work tracking the development of geological formations deep in Burma's Irrawaddy Valley, of slumping down dead tired, foot-blistered, then discovering that he had left his precious notebook behind at the search site. De Terra announced that he was going back to search for it. Teilhard would hear nothing of this. De Terra was in pain; he would go himself. "Deaf to my entreaties," said de Terra, "he pulled on his tennis shoes, called for the guide and vanished with him into the pitch-black night by the light of a pocket-lamp. When he returned some hours later and brought the notebook to my tent, his whole face was beaming with delight." To Teilhard, his was a small gesture of kindness; to de Terra, it was anything but small. "In fact," commented de Terra, "he could hardly have done me a greater service, since the book contained a record of all the finds which we had made and discussed together in preceding weeks."

De Terra attests to another facet of Teilhard's character: "He was devoid of petty jealousies which so often intrude themselves into professional circles. By banishing all such trivial considerations, his daily companionship relieved me, as leader of the expedition, of all kinds of worries. He never insisted on being accorded the privileges to which his status as the guest and senior member of our party really entitled him."

Nothing pleased Teilhard more, de Terra added, than to perform some service which furthered a friend's research. He was an unselfish man.

Teilhard's unselfishness is more than a key to his personality, and thus his professional manners and modes. It is a key also to his spirituality. As conceived and pursued, Teilhard's mission was to open the eyes of the world to "the ever-greater Christ" and the eyes of the Church to the potential within itself for discovering that Christ. It was an unselfish mission, persevered in with obedience and loyalty, and with dignity, despite the many trials to which he was subjected. Teilhard ever declined to take his case to the court of public opinion, even when it was apparent that his requests for publication were being pigeonholed and that he himself was being shunted off into what was hoped would be obscurity. His relationship to his Church was forever characterized by honesty, straightforwardness (attended by deference), and nobility. Given the circumstances—censorship, rejection, exile—his was the patience of a saint, the example of another Job. There were tears, literal tears over what he considered an unjust fate. There was private complaint. But there never was rude, public railing.

He would even endure public scientific embarrassment with heroic magnanimity, refusing to revile the memory of the person who by all indications was responsible for the most painful of humiliations. The humiliation came just a few years before his death, when chemical analyses revealed that one of the peak experiences of his career, the discovery of "primitive man" in a gravel pit of Piltdown Common in southeast

England, derived from a fraud. Teilhard, at the time a theology student at Ore Place in Hastings, had been duped. The dig he assisted on had been "salted" with bones that had been artificially stained and teeth that had been filed or otherwise shaped to simulate human patterns of use. Instead of a true ancestor of modern man, one had an ingenious combination of a human skull, not particularly old, and the jaw of an orangutan. The perpetrator of the fraud, ostensibly, was Charles Dawson, a lawyer and amateur geologist, but also a friend of Teilhard. The fraud went uncertified for some forty years, and Dawson was long since dead when the true story was uncovered. It would have been easy for Teilhard to indulge himself in vituperation. Instead, he chose to make no public statement. He would play the fool, the dupe. He would not excoriate Dawson's memory, though he was hurt, hurt bitterly. He would confide his feelings in a letter to a friend: "I still have trouble believing that Dawson himself perpetrated the fraud. Fantastic though it seems, I would prefer to think that someone else innocently threw the bone fragments from a neighborhood cottage into the ditch. . . . Nevertheless I must admit to you that this new discovery, splendid though it is, spoils one of the happiest memories of my early scientific career."

In his charitableness toward Dawson Teilhard was the very personification of the "Christian love," that evolutive love which he foresaw one day enveloping all races, classes, people. It is that love which, in the fashion of the great mystics of Christian history, reaches out in the one direction to the infinite and intangible God, and in the other to humankind generally in love of neighbor and by activity in and upon the world. It is that love which, as Teilhardian justice would have it, finds explication in the documents of Vatican Council II and particularly the Pastoral Constitution on the Church in the Modern World. It is meet and just that

scholars should be able to look back today from a period of years and discern the Teilhardian spirit in the
Council documents.

Teilhard's love of God and his commitment to the
world are succinctly combined in advice extended in
1950, five years before his death, to a priest-friend undergoing his own trial and his own dark night of the
soul. "I can only offer you my own method of dealing
with the problem," said Teilhard. "Love Christ *fortier*
(the ever-greater Christ) *through men*, and (if I dare
say it) even beyond the hierarchical Church. And in
order to adore and to discover this greater conception
of Divinity, vow yourself to serve the further development of humanity through research. The silent working
of Providence will do the rest."

The advice may have been to a fellow priest, but its
application is to the wider community of believers. It is
advice that finds an alternate expression in *The Divine
Milieu*, Teilhard's "little book of piety" which some
consider the best guide available to contemporary spirituality: "We serve to complete creation even by the
humblest work of our hands. In virtue of the interrela-
tion between matter, soul and Christ, we bring part of
our being which He desires back to God. In whatever
we do . . . we bring to Christ a little fulfillment." This
is the kernel of Teilhard's thought, the cornerstone of
his spirituality.

It may take the duration of creation for people to
grasp Teilhard's ideas completely. It may even be that
his ideas will never win full currency. Teilhard, nevertheless, will remain a man for the Church's every sea-
son: devout, obedient, kind, insightful—and eternally
optimistic by reason of the Teilhardian conviction that
all which began in God must inevitably return to God.

Teilhard himself returned to God on Easter Sunday
of 1955. Was it coincidence, or was it sign that he
should die on the great symbolic feast of his science

and his theology: the feast which in the Teilhardian principle of convergence conveyed to the universe its essential Christic dimension, the Feast of the Risen Christ? In either case, Teilhard's death seems the answer to a prayer . . . *the* prayer spoken in *The Divine Milieu:*

". . . when I feel I am losing hold of myself, absolutely passive in the hands of the great unknown forces that have shaped me, in those dark moments, grant, O God, that I may understand that it is You who are painfully parting the fibers of my being in order to penetrate the very marrow of my substance, and bear me away with You. . . . O divine Energy, ineluctable and vivifying Power, because, of us two, You are infinitely the stronger, it is to You that the role falls of consuming me in the union which should weld us together. Grant me, therefore, something still more precious than the grace for which all the faithful pray. It is not enough that I should die while communicating. Teach me to communicate while dying."

To those who say that Teilhard's death was not sign, the answer may be Teilhard's own words: "Your God is too small." For communicate in death he did. And communicate with the world he continues to do through the legacy of his papers and the example of a saintly life. A quarter century has dimmed neither word nor example. Teilhard de Chardin stands firmly in Christian history as a major figure of the twentieth century, a thinker and a doer, a mover with the strength to withstand adversity and the faith to point himself and the world past dark moments of the present to the certainty of an ultra-tomorrow. He could do this, because he knew that Christ was risen and that God, the Father, was in heaven—or at least at the Omega Point.

# MOTHER TERESA OF CALCUTTA

*Eileen Egan*

At the shrine of the goddess Kali in Calcutta is a caravanserai. It is ivory in color and from its roof rise eight bulbous, fluted cupolas topped by slender spires. The structure is built around a larger inner courtyard, after the manner of the traditional *serai,* or hostel for pilgrims and merchants. Such hostels marked the old Middle East caravan routes and the ancient Silk Route to Asia. This hostel was intended to serve the poorest pilgrims who make their puja, their act of worship, to Kali, goddess of death and destruction. Her image, with its necklace of skulls, stood nearby in its shrine, a squat, silver-domed temple.

It was the least likely place in which to find a Catholic nun, yet it was there that Mother Teresa took me in 1955. It had become a hostel for pilgrims of the ultimate moment, men and women barely alive, picked up from the alleyways and gutters of a scourged city. The small unknown woman, then in her mid-forties, moved with gentle care in a hall filled with raging diseases, of which the all-conquering one was starvation.

The same small woman I had seen leaning over a skeletonized man in the hostel for the dying was, barely a quarter of a century later, the focus of all eyes as she mounted the platform of the Aula Magna of the University of Oslo. Then I had stood frozen with fear as she had stroked the brown, sticklike arm and murmured consoling words. On December 10, 1979, before a king and a hall filled with diplomats, politicians, members of the academy and the press, the same woman, her white cotton sari shining under the spotlights, stood framed against the sunrise mural of Edvard Munch. She had been named as the recipient of the ultimate accolade, the Nobel Prize for Peace.

The anthem of praise for Mother Teresa as the choice for the 1979 Nobel Award had been preceded by world attention never accorded to a nun in history. She had been pictured on the cover of *Time* magazine as an exemplar of a "living Saint." A book on her work in Calcutta by Malcolm Muggeridge had been translated into many languages and a film based on it had been shown around the world. Universities from Cambridge to Yale had vied to present her with honorary degrees. A jury of the world's major religions had voted her the Templeton Prize for Progress in Religion, a prize that brought to the poor as significant a sum as that which accompanied the Nobel Prize. Pope Paul VI had given her the Pope John XXIII Prize for Peace and the Vatican had placed her on their delegation to the World Congress for International Woman's Year. The United Nations had struck a medal depicting her image as a world figure in the struggle against hunger.

The media of the world searched for their most telling encomiums on the announcement of the Nobel Award. The New York *Times* commented editorially that Mother Teresa was a "secular saint," undoubtedly considering it as the very highest encomium. The fact that Mother Teresa's concerns were not secular was indicated at Oslo, when, on the acceptance of the prize, she asked everyone to join her in prayer. The prayer, already distributed to all, including the press, was the peace prayer attributed to the poor man of Assisi, "Lord, make me a channel of your peace . . . where there is hatred, let me sow love . . . for it is in giving that we receive, in pardoning that we are pardoned, and it is in dying that we are born to eternal life."

Communal prayer was certainly a new departure for the Nobel ceremony, but for those of us close to Mother Teresa, this simple act was a sign of the daily reality of her life. It was a life lived in such a way, to quote St. Paul, as "to take every thought captive and make it obey Christ."

Another departure was the lack of a ceremonial banquet. Mother Teresa had accepted the Nobel Award because through it the poor of the world were being recognized. From the Aula Magna we were directed to a simple reception where the Nobel Committee and Mother Teresa could greet the guests in person. The banquet funds, amounting to $7,000, were donated to Mother Teresa, allowing her to feed hundreds of the poor in Calcutta for a year.

In the Aula Magna in Oslo the various strands of Mother Teresa's life came together in those of us invited from Skopje, Yugoslavia, from Calcutta, India, from Palermo, Sicily, and from Europe and the United States.

Skopje, where Mother Teresa was born in 1910, was represented by its Catholic bishop, Nikola Prela. Though a citizen of Yugoslavia, Bishop Prela stated proudly, "I also am Albanian," identifying with Mother Teresa's ancestry and with the sizeable Albanian minority in Yugoslavia. At the time of her birth, Skopje was still in the Ottoman Empire. Minarets pierced the skyline and the calls to prayer brought worshippers to ancient mosques standing on ancient streets. These were, and those that survived the 1963 earthquake still are, among the testimonies to Turkish occupation and long Islamic presence. In one quarter of the city was a busy oriental bazaar. Byzantium left its impress with a large community of Orthodox believers grouped around richly ornamented churches. The Catholic community was a minority, but one possessing the strong sense of identity that is forged by tenacious resistance. Since she took her origins at a meeting place of diverse religions and cultures, it was undoubtedly easier for Mother Teresa to cross cultural boundaries and see the externals of Western Christianity as no more than trappings.

Besides Mother Teresa, there were two other sari-enveloped figures in the hall, invited by the Nobel Committee to be Mother Teresa's companions from Calcutta. They were Sister Agnes and Sister Gertrude, the first two young women to brave the streets of Calcutta with Mother Teresa in 1949, thus becoming the forerunners of the new religious family known as the Missionaries of Charity.

From Palermo, Sicily, came the only surviving member of Mother Teresa's immediate family, her brother, Lazar Bojaxhiu. He had settled in Italy after the Second World War, becoming the representative of a pharmaceutical company. Married to an Italian, he had brought his only child, a daughter. A tall, outgoing man of soldierly carriage, Lazar Bojaxhiu told of life in Skopje: "There were three of us, Age, my oldest sister, then me, and then Agnes, three years younger than I. Agnes Gonxha was 'Mother's' full name." He had caught the habit of calling Mother Teresa "Mother" from the Missionaries of Charity in Rome and Palermo. "Gonxha means flower in Albanian. She was a good-looking, active girl with a beautiful singing voice."

The father, Nikola Bojaxhiu, was a strong Albanian nationalist, while the mother had a deeply religious bent. Her maiden name was Drone Bernai, and her people had come originally from the Venetian region. Drone was another word for flower, Bojaxhiu explained. The household in which Agnes Gonxha grew up was one with a strong sense of values and strict commitment to them. On the mother's side, religious devotion was expressed not only in attendance at church and family worship but in a sober life style marked by charitable care for others. A political thrust on behalf of a long-occupied people entered through the father's influence.

It was a happy, well-ordered, well-provided household. Nikola prospered as a contractor and an importer of food. His firm helped to build the Skopje Theater. Drone would never turn away the needy, and Nikola left funds with her so that she would be ready to help anyone who came to her. The house was a spacious one set in a pleasant garden with flowers and fruit trees. The Bojaxhiu family were also the owners of the adjoining house. Drone did not confine her charitable work to the giving of alms. She visited the sick and brought into her home a woman afflicted with a painful tumor. Since the woman's family would not care for her, Drone gave her shelter and personal nursing. Every evening, the whole family knelt down to recite the rosary.

When Agnes Gonxha was nine years of age, in 1919, the household was visited by bitter tragedy. Nikola's Albanian nationalism had led him into a movement to have the province of Kossovo, inhabited by many Albanians, joined to a greater Albania after the Second World War. He went to a political dinner in Belgrade, leaving home in fine health, a vigorous man of forty-five. He came home a dying man. He was taken, hemorrhaging, to the local hospital, where no surgery could save him. The doctors, and the family, were convinced that he had been poisoned. Following Nikola's death, his business partner plundered the business of its resources, and the family was left with nothing but their shelter.

Only the enterprise of the mother saved the family. She set up a business of selling cloth and locally crafted embroidery and rugs, and it grew by her skill and hard work. Soon managers of Skopje's textile factories were asking her advice on what materials to produce for better sales.

Mother Teresa described her mother as a down-to-earth person who did not countenance the wasting of time. One evening, when the three young people were engaging in small talk that became sillier as the evening wore on, the mother sat listening but saying nothing. She left the room and turned off the main electric switch, plunging the house into darkness. Her comment to her children was that there was no use wasting light so that such foolishness could go on. Mother Teresa reflects this quality in her objection to waste of any kind, of time, of resources or of human gifts. On another occasion, Drone gave her daughter Agnes Gonxha advice that was forever carved on her heart, "Put your hand in His—in His hand—and walk all the way with Him."

Agnes Gonxha saw Lazar on vacation after his mother sent him at the age of twelve to military school in Graz, Austria. Following that, he was accepted for military school in Tirana, capital of free Albania. Kossovo did not become Albanian territory, having been awarded to newly demarcated Yugoslavia. During his times at home, the teen-aged Bojaxhiu found he had different interests from his younger sister. She was occupied in arranging festivals in the little parish church on the same street, singing in the choir, and always busy with some event. Agnes Gonxha and Drone seemed to live in church in those days. Agnes Gonxha was helpful to her schoolmates, often tutoring students from her class in their home. Lazar Bojaxhiu was active in sports and spent much time outside the home with his friends.

"I was more like my father," he related; "'Mother' was more like our own mother. When I see the Sisters in Palermo, I see our mother in her, so strong, and so strict in religious practice."

Agnes Gonxha wrote to Lazar when he was made a lieutenant at the age of twenty-one, to tell him that at the age of eighteen, she had made a decision about her future. She shocked him with the news that she was going to become a nun, a missionary in India. He wrote to ask how a lovely young girl could give up her life and go so far away, probably never to see her family in her whole life. Agnes Gonxha wrote back explaining her decision, one sentence of which her brother remembered word for word, "You are serving a king of 2,000,000 people. I shall serve the king of the whole world."

While in the state school, or gymnasium, of Skopje, Agnes Gonxha joined the Sodality of the Blessed Virgin Mary. At the Sodality meetings, letters were read from the Yugoslav missionaries of the Society of Jesus who had become part of the Bengal mission in 1925. It was these letters that set her spirit on fire, turning her mind toward the East. They moved her to leave a close family for a faraway mission. They were the seed of her calling to Bengal.

Also at Oslo was another strand of Mother Teresa's life, the Co-Workers, a lay group motivated by her spiritual vision. Mrs. Ann Blaikie of England, formerly a Calcuttan, was there as head, or International Link, of the loosely organized, world-wide movement numbering about two hundred thousand. By her side was Jacqueline de Decker from Belgium, able to move around with the help of complicated steel braces. Already a lay missionary in India, she had wanted to join Mother Teresa in 1948, but was prevented by ill health. The contact with Mother Teresa had never been broken. Jacqueline de Decker became the Link with Sick and Suffering Co-Workers, giving each the name of a missionary of charity somewhere in the world for whom prayers and sufferings could be offered. Co-Workers were invited from various countries in Western Europe and the writer from the United States. Even in the rush of events surrounding the Nobel Award, the evening Nobel Lecture (distinct from the acceptance speech), the services at the Lutheran and Catholic cathedrals, the torchlight procession through the icy, starry Norway night and the televised interviews, Mother Teresa found time to be sequestered with the Co-Workers. They met in prayer and in thanksgiving for what Mother Teresa called the real Nobel gift, the gift of recognition of the poor of the world.

In October 1955, Mother Teresa took me through the thronged street leading to the caravanserai that had become a hostel for the dying. Cows arrogantly edged men and women off the pavement and beggars smiled with brown-red teeth after spitting betel-nut juice in the gutter. Hawkers came out of their little kiosks to sell brightly colored images of Kali. Others sold leaves and marigolds which the devout could take as an offering to the goddess, taking care not to breathe the scent from the flowers on their way to the shrine. Some of the people resting on the pavement must have been Kali's pilgrims, since they had a blotch of red on their foreheads. It was not betel juice, I was told, but fresh blood from the body of a goat sacrificed that morning in the temple courtyard. Blood sacrifice, reflecting a primordial religious rite, lived on at Kali's shrine. The air was heavy with the smoke sent up by the funeral pyres of Hindus being cremated at the nearby burning ghat, the Kalighat.

The door to which Mother Teresa brought me was outlined with the fanciful tracery of the Mogul scalloped arch. I looked up to see some lettering in Bengali script, and over that the fateful words, "Home for the

Destitute Dying, *Nirmal Hriday."* Over all were the words, "Corporation of Calcutta."

When we entered the immense, high-ceilinged hall, I found myself in a dropped cement walkway, between parapets raised on both sides to a height of somewhat over two feet. About sixty figures lay on pallets, thirty on each side, their heads against the walls and their feet against the walkway. The pallets were placed on metal stands, hardly above the cement floor. A sister, a large apron over her sari, was laboriously feeding a prone man, gently turning his head so that he would not suffocate. She kept drying his chin and neck as one would do to a tiny infant. Behind his head was an empty tin slot. A slot was placed behind each man, containing a record of all that could be found out about him. This man must have just been brought in, too close to dying to tell anything about himself, ready to pass out of the world in total anonymity, with no one to call him by his name.

I had already seen men and women, and even children, who seemed not far from death in the *bustees,* the collections of mud-floored huts at the city's outskirts, and in Sealdah Station where more than a thousand recent refugees settled in unimaginable squalor. But there they would be dying one by one, and I would not be there when they fought for their last breath. Here, on both sides of me, the dying were lying side by side in long rows. Some were barely conscious and I wondered what dreams, what visions they might be harboring as they slipped out of life. Mother Teresa sat down on the parapet to take a man's hand in hers. He smiled and tried without success to raise his head. She stepped on the parapet to kneel and talk quietly to a man having difficulty breathing. Sometimes she would just listen and stroke a wasted arm or place her strong hand on a head as if in blessing. Once she slipped into English to talk to a man who must have been Anglo-Indian.

I felt that among the men in the hall there must have been all the diseases known to man. The open, infected sores, the cavernous cheeks, the faces with the terrible grin of death already upon them, paralyzed me. But what was heart-stopping was that, as Mother Teresa could not stop at every pallet, some hands were held out to me.

Fear held me frozen.

In an identical hall, housing almost as many women, young sisters were chatting as they washed worn faces and combed grizzly hair. Again, Mother Teresa went from one to the other, calling out a name and sitting down to talk or listen, and calling the attention of the sisters to some need or other voiced by the women. Seeing me as I walked behind Mother Teresa, even the weakest used their waning strength to wave to me. It was a vain attempt to find human consolation. I stood gazing at them, unable even to touch their fingers. I began to be inundated by shame as well as fear, but I wanted to be sure that nothing would prevent my leaving for Vietnam in a few days.

I commented to Mother Teresa that there must be every disease known to humankind in those two halls.

"No," she answered matter-of-factly, "the Brahmin priests said that no lepers could be brought here. They are right. We have obeyed that to the letter."

*Nirmal Hriday,* Bengali for "Immaculate Heart," had been opened for the destitute dying, she informed me, in 1952. I wondered how she and the sisters could come there day after day. Did they not want at times to turn away?

Mother Teresa said many things to me during those days in 1955, but one thing branded itself deep in my psyche. It expressed her vision of her work and the ground of conviction behind it.

"How could we turn away from Jesus? Each one is Jesus, only Jesus in a distressing disguise.

"Sometimes we meet Jesus rejected and covered with filth in the gutter. Sometimes we find Jesus stuffed into a drain, or moaning with the pain of sores or rotting with gangrene—or even screaming from the agony of a broken back. The most distressing disguise calls for even more love from us."

I soon saw how the lepers fared in Calcutta. They were left to themselves. After walking with Mother Teresa through the dirt-covered alleys of a number of bustees, we came to a bustee in Dhappa in the middle of which was a *pipal* tree. The acceptance of Mother Teresa was complete, was in fact so reverent that she moved with resolute speed to prevent people from bending to touch her feet.

Under the pipal tree was a whitewashed stone with the painted image of a monkey. It was Hanuman, the monkey deity, one of the thousands of deities in the Hindu pantheon. Here no one bent to touch her feet, but the first woman we met joined her palms in the traditional greeting. The fingers were no more than thick, ulcerated stumps. We were in one of the most squalid, the most desolate bustees of all, a nest of lepers. Mother Teresa related that the leprosarium serving Calcutta had been closed down; leprosy patients, often driven out by their families, congregated together in their own communities, leaving them only to beg at the mosques, shrines, and churches of the city.

The people came out of their dark, windowless shacks and stood surrounding us. Mother Teresa joined her hands to give the greeting and many who returned it raised one claw-like hand to the other. The clawed hand is one sign of the disease. A man with hideous excrescences on his nose and cheeks said, "Namaskar," and leaned close to Mother Teresa to tell her something. She did not flinch but put her head near his to

listen. Leprosy was the first dread disease that entered
my consciousness as a child raised on biblical tales.
Jesus, I thought, Jesus in his most distressing disguise.
It was that vision of Jesus, lived by Mother Teresa, and
lighting up the darkest corners of what has been called
the "slum of the world" that brought me back repeat-
edly to Calcutta and forged a link that continued over
the years. There was the opportunity, as a staff
member of the American Catholic overseas aid agency
said, to increase concern for India and to support the
channeling of more life-saving foods from the mountain of American abundance to those perishing from
hunger.

The acceptance of Mother Teresa by the poor, as
well as by most other groups in Calcutta, was extraordinary, but more extraordinary was the action of the
city fathers in giving her and her sisters the right to
work in the precincts of one of the most revered of
Hindu shrines. The unexampled act arose out of the
special character of the sisters and of their founder.

At the time of the decision by the Corporation of
Calcutta, as the city fathers are called, to turn over the
pilgrim's hostel at Kali's Temple to Mother Teresa, all
the sisters were of Indian nationality. They wore the
Indian sari, as did ordinary Indian women, only in
their case, the garment was all-enveloping, to cover the
body and the nun's shorn head. Their founder was Indian by choice, having been accepted for Indian citizenship after India emerged as a free nation in 1947.
When I first met Mother Teresa, her skin ochred by the
sun and her eyes gray-brown, I thought she might be a
Kashmiri or Punjabi. She spoke Bengali and Hindi
fluently and her accent in speaking English could not
be placed. Her love for the people around her and her
respect for their traditions could not be missed.

The reverence for self-abnegation and holiness is

deep in Indian society. While the holy man, who lives on alms freely given even by the poor, has customarily gone through the life cycle of apprentice or student, then householder and father, before he reaches the stage of renunciation and celibacy, the young women around Mother Teresa had telescoped the life cycle. The fact that young Indians could commit themselves to celibacy for Jesus elicited admiration. Celibate priests and nuns, dressed as they would in the West and living as close as possible to Western ways, had served Indian missions for centuries, but this had seemed related to an alien tradition. After 1950, the Indian community saw a growing group of their own people, while still in their youth, committing themselves to lifelong celibacy. They ignored caste and class as Gandhi had done in his ashrams. They adopted the clothing of the people and spoke to them in their own tongues. When they met in their simple chapel, they left their sandals outside and squatted on the floor as did worshippers in Hindu holy places. The usual trappings of Western Christianity were missing. Mother Teresa had laid them aside. What she had treasured was the basic message of Jesus to his followers, the message of love that brooks no barriers in validating the divine spirit in the other. The sari-enveloped Mother Teresa and the missionaries of charity did not carry on their good works of teaching and healing behind strong walls. One of Mother Teresa's first aims was to break down the walls and go out to the poor rather than stay in one place and wait for the poor to come to them. Their schools were often held in the open air, as were the "leper stations" which brought specialists and the latest medications to nests of lepers like that at Dhappa.

While the work of other Christian missionaries, whether Catholic or Protestant, was related in small or large measure to evangelizing, the Missionaries of Charity, in dealing with the needy of other religious traditions, allowed their ministration to be their message. They became known in Bengal as *Prem Prochariko,* the Preachers of Love—who do not preach. Mother Teresa and the sisters were discovering the simple fact that no one objects to being treated as if he or she were the Savior.

While the letters from the Yugoslav missioners, read at the meetings of the Sodality of Mary, were the immediate spur to a high school girl in Skopje to become a missionary nun, a seed had been planted earlier. From the age of twelve, Agnes Gonxha Bojaxhiu, growing up in a household led by a devout and clear-minded mother, knew she wanted to give her life to the service of Christ. She did not know what form this service would take until at eighteen she was moved to join the missions in Bengal. She wrote to the Jesuit Fathers asking how this could be done. They told her of the long Bengali service of the Sisters of Loreto.

The route to Bengal for the young Albanian girl in Skopje, capital of Yugoslav Macedonia, led through Ireland. The link of Ireland with India was of long duration, since generations of dispossessed young Irishmen "took the King's shilling" to serve the same British raj which had colonized both Ireland and India. Beginning in 1842, an order of Catholic nuns, the Irish branch of the Institute of Mary, had been active in Bengal, chiefly teaching and caring for orphans. They were called the Sisters of Loreto from a shrine of Loreto at their motherhouse in Rathfarnham in Dublin. It was in 1928, at Rathfarnham, that Agnes Gonxha was accepted as the first step toward Bengal. Already fluent in the Albanian and Serbo-Croatian tongues, she now confronted the English language. She remained in Ireland for six weeks.

Early in 1929, Agnes Gonxha Bojaxhiu arrived in

Calcutta, capital of Bengal, and did not leave the province for 31 years. Her novitiate training period was spent in Darjeeling, two hundred and fifty miles north of Calcutta in the foothills of the Himalayas, from which Mt. Everest could be glimpsed. She made her first vows as a Sister of Loreto on May 24, 1931, taking as her patron a nun canonized just six years earlier, St. Thérèse, known as the "Little Flower." "Not the big St. Teresa of Avila," she always explained, "but the little one." Her final vows were made in Darjeeling in 1937.

Sister Teresa taught at St. Mary's School in Entally, Calcutta, later becoming its principal. She was given charge of an Indian order of sisters, the Daughters of St. Ann, who were affiliated with the Loreto sisters.

"I taught geography for many years," she told me. "I never thought I would visit so many of the places I taught about."

During the nineteen years that Sister Teresa taught as a Loreto nun behind the walls of the Entally compound, India went through the convulsions leading to freedom. Gandhi's nonviolent campaigns, including the historic Salt March, involved more and more of India's people in resistance and in resulting massive arrests. Without their consent, the Indian people were swept into the limitless violence of the Second World War when Britain declared war on their behalf. Bengal suffered most disastrously. The dislocation brought on by war with its all-consuming priorities and the sequestering of river craft by which rice was delivered from the paddylands contributed to one of history's most destructive famines. The 1943 Bengal famine took the lives of at least 2,000,000 people, perhaps as many as 4,000,000 to 5,000,000, according to Indian figures. The streets of Mother Kali's city were filled with the starving who flocked from the rural areas to the city's soup kitchens. They perished in such numbers that the smoke from the burning ghats was continuous.

In 1946, another disaster struck Calcutta. In the Hindu-Muslim conflict that preceded partition and the freedom of the Indian subcontinent, a "Direct Action Day" was declared by the Muslim League. Bengal's population, like Calcutta's, was almost evenly divided between Muslims and Hindus. Direct Action Day became the occasion for communal violence, the term for violence between the two religious groups, and once unleashed, it bathed the streets of Calcutta in blood. The city was brought to a standstill. As principal of St. Mary's School, Sister Teresa went outside the compound in search of supplies after all deliveries had stopped. Death was everywhere; violence had shaken the city to its foundations. Whenever Mother Teresa referred to Direct Action Day, August 16, 1946, she always called it, as Calcuttans do, the "Day of the Great Killing." And whenever she mentioned it, her face clouded over with deep sadness.

What had happened was an explosion of Hindu-Muslim violence that eventually took at least a million lives, darkening both sides of new-made borders in a sea of blood. On Calcutta's streets, men and women were pierced with *lathis,* metal-shod rods, and left to bleed to death; shops were set afire with their owners inside; sewers were flooded with the bodies tossed into them. People hid themselves from the marauders in utter terror. It was such explosions of violence that gave rise to one of the most tragic exchanges of populations in history; about 16,000,000 men, women, and children became refugees, fleeing from their homes to take refuge in either India or newly created Pakistan. At least 4,000,000 Hindus streamed into west Bengal, India, from the eastern part of the province which was made part of Pakistan. The day of India's freedom, August 15, 1947, was thus a time of agony for millions of helpless, denuded people.

I asked Mother Teresa if the Day of the Great

Killing had impelled her to come from behind convent walls to bring mercy to streets that had known such mercilessness. She replied in the negative. The impulsion came from something that occurred less than a month later when she was traveling north to make her retreat.

"It was on the tenth of September 1946," she related, "in the train that took me to Darjeeling, the hill station in the Himalayas. It was then that I heard the call of God. The message was quite clear. I was to leave the convent and help the poor while living among them. It was an order. I knew where I belonged. I did not know how to get where I belonged."

The Missionaries of Charity call September 10 "Inspiration Day," and they consider their society an answer to the special call given to their founder on that day.

Mother Teresa has been asked in my presence if she had ever had a vision or if her work was inspired by visions. Her reply was, "No, I have not had a vision. I do not have visions." It was simply a call, or as she described it, "a call within a call," since she was already a religious in vows.

In the conviction that her vocation was entering a new phase, she asked for permission to remain as a nun but to leave the enclosure of the convent. The Mother General of Loreto gave a loving assent, perhaps in the remembrance that the Loreto sisters, descended from the Institute of Mary, were suppressed in 1630 precisely because its founder wanted to dispense with enclosure for greater freedom in teaching poor and rich. Church authorities also gave her permission for exclaustration. She often said that leaving the Sisters of Loreto was the greatest sacrifice she was ever called upon to make, greater even than breaking away from her family in Skopje. Nevertheless, she took leave of her religious

family. On August 16, 1948, two years after the Day of
the Great Killing, she walked out of the Loreto convent
alone. She could not have known that her life was to
become so inextricably woven with the agonies of Calcutta that the name of the city became affixed to her
name; nor could she have pictured a time when, on announcement of the Nobel Award, the chief minister of
the province, a Communist, was to call her the Mother
of Bengal.

The lonely nun was given hospitality by the American Medical Mission sisters at Holy Family Hospital in
Patna, in the neighboring state of Bihar. For three
months she took a concentrated course in basic nursing
from the sister-doctors and sister-nurses of the order. In
December 1948, she boarded the train for the three
hundred mile journey to Calcutta, to the streets on
which she knew she belonged. She was thirty-eight
years of age. Since she would be living with the poor,
she chose the cheap cotton sari of the poor. It was
wrapped around her head so that it approximated a
nun's head covering. On her left shoulder a small
crucifix was attached with a safety pin. She wore a pair
of sandals given her by the sisters at Patna. She had
five rupees.

The Little Sisters of the Poor allowed her to stay at
their home for the aged. Since she had been a teacher,
she started by teaching the school-less children in Moti
Jihl, the bustee near St. Mary's School. It was in that
bustee that her students, members of the Sodality of
the Blessed Virgin Mary, had served the poor.

Mother Teresa took me to see Moti Jihl on an early
visit. Moti Jihl, literally Pearl Lake, had grown around
a scum-covered, stagnant pond from which the resi-
dents drew all their water for drinking and washing.
Naked children were playing around it, some with coal
blacking under their eyes as protection against the

sun's glare. A number had stomachs that protruded like shining brown balloons under pathetically thin rib cages.

"Here was the first of our schools," she related. "You see that plum tree over there?"

On the far side of the pond was a single tree, thinly leaved and no taller than a man.

"I went to the mothers and fathers and asked if they wanted their children to learn. They sent them to me. The first day I had just a few children, perhaps five. I sat on a chair under that tree and the children gathered round me on the ground. Soon more than forty came every day. They were such good children. They wanted to learn.

"I had no money for slates or chalk, or a blackboard, so when it came time to write something, I used a stick to mark it on the ground where the children were sitting. Soon we had a few benches and we could have continued very nicely until monsoon time. When some of my students joined me, we rented two huts and we did not need to worry about the monsoon after that."

I realized that the day on which Mother Teresa started the open-air school in Moti Jihl was December 21, 1948, a few days after she had stepped into the abyss of a new life with utter faith that she was answering a call.

Between the time that she started the school and the day her first student joined her, Mother Teresa made her way alone to Moti Jihl, about an hour's walk from the Little Sisters of the Poor. She carried her food and would look for a quiet place to eat it. Once she knocked at the door of a convent (unnamed) and asked if she could come inside to take her food. She was told to go around to the back and was left to eat her sparse midday meal under the back stairs like a beggar. Such a reception was not too surprising, since she was a strange sight on Calcutta's streets, a lone nun

who was Indianized not only in dress but in becoming
a citizen of India. Even one of her strongest supporters
in later years, a Yugoslav Jesuit priest, told of his reaction to her new garb, saying, "We thought she was
cracked."

Mother Teresa wrote of those early days, "God
wants me to be a lonely nun, laden with the poverty of
the Cross. The poverty of the poor is so hard. . . .
When I was going and going till my legs and arms
were paining, I was thinking how they have to suffer to
get food and shelter."

Three months after her arrival in Calcutta, Subashini
Das, who had been a boarder at St. Mary's School from
the age of nine, came to join Mother Teresa. It was the
feast of St. Joseph, March 19, 1949. By then, Mother
Teresa had been given the use of an upper room in a
large old house owned by a Catholic family on Creek
Lane. By Easter 1949, Magdalena Gomes, a student
who had come from a Catholic family in Dacca, India,
but evangelized hundreds of years earlier by Portu-
guese missioners, joined them. Both exchanged their
former dress for cotton saris and went with Mother
Teresa to Moti Jihl.

It had been a searing shock for her students when a
greatly loved teacher had suddenly left a boarding
school where she had influenced many lives. They had
been waiting to hear of her whereabouts.

Subashini Das, who took Mother Teresa's first name
as Sister Agnes, recalled that during the years of the
Second World War, Mother Teresa took on much extra
work. She taught almost every subject in addition to
geography, but especially English and religion. "She
taught religion in such a wonderful way," Sister Agnes
related, "that everything came alive for us. We felt the
love of Jesus and his sacrifices for us, and the beauty of
sacrificing for Him. She taught it in our own language.
There were many vocations from her classes, to the

Carmelites and the Daughters of St. Ann as well as to Loreto. I had wanted to become a nun and serve the poor. I come from a modest family and I did not see that I would be giving up anything if I entered one of the orders in Calcutta. It was not until Mother Teresa began to work that I knew what I wanted to do."

Magdalena Gomes, who became Sister Gertrude and continued her medical studies in the Missionaries of Charity, recalled, "She took care of us personally. When we were ill, she stayed up to nurse us. She did everything, even looking after our food. I often wondered how much sleep she could get. Once, when I was ill, it was Mother Teresa who took me to hospital."

"At Creek Lane," Sister Agnes explained, "we lived as nuns, but without a rule at first. We felt sure that our way would be recognized, maybe soon, maybe not so soon. But it would happen."

Within a few months, a dozen young women came to join the "way." The upper room served by turns as refectory, chapel, and dormitory. More rooms in the rambling home were given to the band of young Indian girls led by Mother Teresa. By the end of 1949, the band numbered twenty-seven. On October 7, 1950, Archbishop Ferdinand Perier of Calcutta announced their recognition as a diocesan congregation under the title of the Missionaries of Charity. A house had been found on a lane leading from noisy Lower Calcutta Road, and this became the motherhouse.

When, much later, I was asked to write a short account of the congregation for the leaflet of the lay Co-Workers, Mother Teresa asked me to include the following words: In the choice of works, there was neither planning nor preconceived ideas. We started our work as the sufferings of the people called us. God showed us what to do.

There was no preconceived idea in starting the most

dramatic work, that of gathering the dying from the streets and gutters. There was a woman lying on the street gnawed at by rats, and Mother Teresa picked her up and took her to the hospital. The hospital refused to take her in, so in Mother Teresa's words, "I stood there until they admitted her."

Mother Teresa picked up many men and women and would use the rupees donated for her work to hire a rickshaw or taxi for the trip to the nearest hospital. Taxi drivers would often refuse a poor man full of sores and filth or a woman covered with rags and crawling with maggots or ants. Even when Mother Teresa managed to get them to the doors of the hospital, they were, like as not, refused, no matter how long Mother Teresa stood her ground. Since the arrival of the first million refugees in 1947, there had been a steady stream of refugees from across a border designed to separate religious communities. The newcomers brought their destitution to Calcutta and the hospitals were so overcrowded that patients were cared for in the hallways and any unused space. In an emergency, Mother Teresa borrowed a workman's wheelbarrow and wheeled a sick, untended man to a hospital. In a sense, one could see the Hostel for the Dying rising from that wheelbarrow.

Not willing to allow rejected human beings to perish in the gutter, Mother Teresa rented a room in Moti Jihl, near the school.

"We could do no more than give our people a human death instead of letting them die like animals in the gutter," she said.

Soon, Calcutta's destitute dying were being lovingly cared for in two stifling, dirt-floored rooms. They died in greater peace than they had known while alive. But there was no space for many others who breathed their last in gutters and alleys around the city. Mother Teresa went to the municipality to ask for a place where they could be brought for care by the sisters. The health officer took her to the pilgrims' hostel adjoining Kali's Temple. It was empty. He offered it to Mother Teresa. In twenty-four hours, the patients from Moti Jihl were transferred to the caravanserai.

"I was happy to have this place," Mother Teresa said, "because it is a place of devotion for our people."

One wondered if it had been the proximity of the burning ghats that had moved the health officer to make this particular site available as a hostel for the dying. One wondered also about the strange providence that had brought a Catholic nun, whom the world recognized as a channel of merciful love, in juxtaposition to a goddess of destruction. Yet what Kali stands for is the destruction of all that is dross, and she is seen as the Divine Mother. The Kali Yuga, the age of Kali that is supposed to come upon the world, will be a time when evil will be purged away by destruction, much like the "end time" envisioned by apocalyptic thinkers. After the Nobel Award, a poem in an Indian magazine was addressed to "Ma Teresa, Mother of Calcutta." Ma, "Mother" is a reminder of the way the goddess Kali is addressed, "Kali Ma," Mother Kali. Teresa Ma and Kali Ma, could this juxtaposition be an accident?

In time, I became accustomed to Kalighat, the name most often used for the Hostel for the Dying, but actually the name of the whole area of South Calcutta around Kali's temple and the nearby cremation place. This stands on a tributary of the holy Ganges, where the ashes from the funeral pyres are cast.

As I made my way with Mother Teresa or one of the sisters to the pallet of a woman fighting for breath or a man from whose nose worms were crawling, I envisioned a collision of values above their heads. A man snatched from death on the open street, cleansed, nourished, and cared for with unstinting and seemingly

excessive love, turned with incredulity to Mother
Teresa: "I have lived like an animal in the gutter, but I
am dying loved and cared for." He could not have
known that to Mother Teresa he was no less than the
Savior, and the spittle and stench of the gutter no more
than a distressing disguise.

The amazement with which the homeless and
shunned people reacted to their rescue and care was
shared by the general population which observed it. To
the Hindu, death is seen in the context of reincar-
nation, in which the living principle transmigrates from
one habitation to another. Death is seen as the time
when the snake sheds its skin, an outworn garment, so
that the snake itself may move on in the wheel of rein-
carnation to any branch of living creation. The skin,
the human body, is simply being vacated. Death, like
birth, is seen as a time of pollution.

The person dying of some dread disease, or abandoned and untended on the street, is living out his
karma, the immutable law of cause and effect in the
moral world. This fate has come to pass because of actions in this or a previous existence. In the Hindu tradition, the sufferer tends to be robbed of his dignity since
guilt is imputed to him. This accounts for a lack of dy-
namic action on the part of the observer and for the
striking resignation on the part of the sufferer. In addition, if a person is seen lying on the street, there may
be the gulf of caste between him and the passerby, a
gulf still not bridged by the example of Gandhi or the
Indian constitution.

"What dreadful thing is he guilty of," Hindus ask of
Christ on the Cross, "to deserve that degree of suffering?"

Mother Teresa and her sisters were showing forth a
mystery for which there was no key but Christ on the
Cross, a Christ suffering innocently and willingly for
the sins of humankind. Though in the Christian tradi-

tion there may be a connection between sin and suffering, there is also innocent suffering, and this redemptive suffering is the very heart of the Christian message. One cannot argue back from a hideous disease or lamentable fate to make a judgment on the guilt of the person undergoing them.

Mother Teresa's vision of the street, and of those lying upon it, collided with that of the spirituality around her. She imputed no guilt to the suffering people but viewed them as bathed in the light of the Incarnation. They were inhabited by the Holy Spirit of God, worthy of the same love that would be poured out on Jesus. From each she heard the words of Jesus, "I am the hungry one; I am the homeless one; I am the one naked but for a few rags; I am the thirsty one; I am the suffering one; I am the one imprisoned by want and ignorance." The response of the Christian to Jesus so disguised is related to salvation, to whether one is united forever with Jesus without his human disguise.

The collision above the heads of the dying people in Kalighat arose out of the collision between immutable karma and belief in remission, and that between the reincarnational and incarnational view of humankind. The words of T. S. Eliot in *Preludes* came to mind. Mother Teresa "had such a vision of the street/As the street hardly understands."

Other responses called into being by the sufferings of the people soon spread out over Calcutta in sixty centers. A Children's Home, *Shishu Bhavan*, for "throwaway" children was set up on Lower Circular Road close to the motherhouse. Mother and child clinics brought first aid and long-term healing to the neediest bustees. Schools were opened for children who would otherwise be chained for life to illiteracy. After the sisters had a functioning school with at least a hundred pupils, the Corporation would construct a school build-

ing. A school for the children of lepers, many of them
"untainted," to use the common term, was started in
Dhappa. Beginning as usual with the use of poor
means, the sisters rented a few rooms after holding the
first classes in the open air. I went with Mother Teresa
to visit the children. When she asked them to hold up
their hands, I could hear her passing sentence on the
little ones as she noted blunted fingers or telltale white
patches. The children spoke three of the Indian
tongues, since leprosy patients, after being rejected by
their families, migrate to the anonymity of the cities. A
gift of a mobile clinic by Catholic Relief Services per-
mitted Mother Teresa to organize open-air treatment
days for leper communities by which the victims of the
disease could at least be rendered noninfectious. Centers where lepers could learn crafts, and even have
their own homes, were soon opened. It was not long
before all Calcutta was involved. Early Co-Workers
asked the public to have a part in the campaign against
leprosy by contributing to an annual collection. The
appeal was: "Touch the Leper with Your Compassion."

Mother Teresa left India for the first time in 31 years
in 1960. The National Council of Catholic Women of
the United States accepted my suggestion that she be
invited to talk at their convention in Las Vegas, Ne-
vada. When I met her there, I had to explain why a
ripple of laughter greeted her mention of this destination on her journey from Asia. She had spoken before
small groups in Calcutta, but now she faced thousands
of women.

She told them, "I have never spoken in public before. This is the first time, and to be here with you and
to be able to tell you of the love story of God's mercy
for the poorest of the poor—it is a grace of God." After
thanking American Catholics for their ever-increasing
aid, she told them that she was not going to ask them

for further aid. She explained her complete dependence on the providence of God, once people knew of the needs of their fellow human beings. "I don't beg. I have not begged from the time we started the work. But I go to the people—the Hindus, the Mohammedans and the Christians—and I tell them: 'I have come to give you a chance to do something beautiful for God!' And the people, they want to do something beautiful for God and they come forward." She told the women that at the ten year mark of the Missionaries of Charity, there were 119 Sisters, all but 3 of whom were Indian.

Mother Teresa's goal was Rome, where she had a crucial mission for the Society, and I accompanied her to Europe. During our visit to Germany, we drove to the Dachau concentration camp. A look of terrible pain captured her face as she stood on the blood-soaked acres and we talked about the concentration-camp world of Europe during the Second World War. She lowered her head. She might have been praying. "That human beings could do these things to other human beings," she said at last.

In the Vatican, as we made our way through the corridors, I sensed for the first time the awe that was to greet her on later travels. The words "Madre Fondatrice" speeded us on until we were in the presence of two cardinals, Amleto Cicognani and Gregory Agagianian. Mother Teresa was making formal application for recognition of the Missionaries of Charity as a Society of Pontifical Right. The cardinals placed us on a red plush settee as they perused the document that Mother Teresa had had me type that morning. They asked about the number of sisters, their traning, the types of work, and especially about the fourth vow of "wholehearted, free service to the poorest of the poor." Mother Teresa told them of a life "woven about the Eucharist" and totally dependent on the providence of

God. They pored over the sisters' prayer book, printed in English as the common language of a multilingual society.

Following this, there was a moving family reunion with the brother she had not seen since 1928. Lazar Bojaxhiu brought his wife Maria and his daughter Aggi. They shared the pain of an almost total lack of communication with the mother and elder sister who had moved to Tirana, Albania, during the Second World War. Drone and Age Bojaxhiu were living in an officially atheist nation where a bishop and a priest were executed for unauthorized spiritual care. Despite efforts to bring them out of Albania, both died in Tirana.

The reply to the petition put before the two cardinals in November 1960 was made in February 1965. Undoubtedly, the petition set in motion by Mother Teresa in person was succeeded by careful study before the Vatican made its decision. Mother Teresa was informed in 1965 that the Missionaries of Charity was recognized as a Society of Pontifical Right, a new family within the Catholic Church, and one that could move beyond diocesan boundaries to work anywhere in the world.

Mother Teresa was now a Mother Founder, but one like none other. She never used *Reverend* Mother; her title was simply "Mother," and she considered herself the spiritual mother of the young women joining the society. She asked them "to love Christ with undivided love in chastity, through freedom of poverty, in total surrender in obedience, and wholehearted and free service to the poorest of the poor."

The use of small means permeated all the works of the society as well as the manner of life of the sisters. When the Missionaries of Charity established houses in the poorer quarters of a score of Indian cities, Mother

Teresa had to begin regular visitations. Given a free pass for Indian Railways, she often traveled by night to save time and would sleep on the luggage rack. She offered to be a helper or stewardess on Indian Airlines in return for free flights. Eventually, she was awarded a free air pass.

Soon the Missionaries of Charity were moving out into the world at the invitation of local bishops, invitations often initiated by heads of government, as happened in Mexico. Wherever they go, in their little teams of six, each one carries her bedroll with three saris inside it, and her copy of the society's constitution. They speed like arrows to the most anguished corners of the planet. I have seen them face human agony and need from Calcutta to Lima, Peru; from Tabora, Tanzania, to the Australian outback where they live and work with aboriginals; from Benares, where the devout come to die near them by the sacred Ganges, to the slums of Rome; and from the interior of Venezuela to New York City's South Bronx. They find acceptance even in Yemen where Christians have been absent for eight hundred years. Teams are working in over two hundred foundations with Sisters drawn from a total of about two thousand Missionaries of Charity. Novitiates in Rome, Calcutta, and Manila are filled with young women preparing themselves for a life among the poor. The Missionaries of Charity gained a male branch when an Australian Jesuit priest, trained in India, founded it in 1963. The first work of the brothers was to take charge of the men's ward of the Hostel for the Dying. The Co-Workers, a term taken from Gandhi, were formally organized in 1969. Besides cooperating with the Missionaries of Charity, small groups of lay people practice the spirituality of Mother Teresa in faraway regions, like northwestern Canada, where sisters and brothers are not likely to work.

The sisters' expressed aim is "to quench the infinite

thirst of Jesus Christ for love by the profession of the
evangelical counsels and wholehearted free service to
the poorest of the poor, according to the teaching and
life of Our Lord in the Gospel, revealing in a unique
way the Kingdom of God." On arriving at a new mission, they immediately choose a room, however simple,
to serve as a chapel. They put up a crucifix and next to
it the words, "I THIRST."

When the sisters were asked to work in the more
economically developed world of Europe, Australia,
and the United States, they found a different kind of
poverty, which Mother Teresa described as "a poverty
of the spirit, of loneliness, and of being unwanted.
That," she said, "is the worst disease in the world
today." The sisters have a mission over and above the
works of mercy that serve the body. Their aim must be,
"To clothe the naked, not only with clothes but with
human dignity; to give shelter to the shelterless, not
only a shelter made of bricks, but a heart that understands, that covers, that loves."

Does the spirituality of Mother Teresa, which has
touched people from so many cultural, religious, and
national traditions in our nuclear-fragile century, have
some special qualities? Can one find some strands in it
that throw light on why a radical and often inchoate
hunger for holiness finds sustenance in her?

As can be seen in the work for the least in Calcutta,
her vision validates the spirit of the divine in each
human creature. In order to see the divine in "the
other," it is necessary to recognize the divine in one's
own being. In this century, which has seen millions of
human beings gassed and cremated and others destroyed by bombs from on high, the value of each
human life has been put in question for many. Even in
peacetime, millions of human beings, like so much use-
less debris, are thrust over borders, which are somehow
considered sacred, to become refugees. Their survival,

whether in India, Western Europe or Africa (which has been called the "continent of refugees") depends on the compassion of others. Where this is absent, they perish.

As the twentieth century wore on, and the power at the heart of the atom was harnessed for destruction, human beings realized that they could be expunged like so many insects in the organized massacres of modern war. All around them, in the actuality of the depersonalization of modern life, as well as its explosions of hatred and its threat of extinction, there is the pervasive "bad news" of their expendability, of their ultimate unimportance.

A little woman brings them "good news," the news of their infinite value, a value that contradicts all the messages that the world may give them. Her message is a reminder of the aim of the blind poet who sought to "justify God's ways to man." She tells them from every platform open to her that God really loves the world, and that the works of love of the sisters around the world are only a way of revealing the love God has for them. She has become a sign of a loving God, a living sign of a loving God. People seem to need an alternative vision of the world from that of a planet ready to self-destruct; they need a view of the world in which it and they are fulfilling a purpose, a world created by a loving Creator whose love still streams forth over his creation.

Seeing God as a loving Creator, Mother Teresa has utter trust in His providence. This is perhaps her outstanding characteristic as a person and as a Christian. She asks others to dare to live by this trust. This means emptying oneself—of excess possessions and concerns, of pride and dependence on one's own powers—so that the spirit and power of God may have room to enter in.

Taking the Gospel literally, she sees it as a duty to work toward love of all human creatures, "who have come forth from the same loving hand of God." She takes Jesus literally in his identification with the least, for she keeps repeating, "He can neither deceive nor be deceived."

Mother Teresa's all-absorbing concern is with holiness, which to her consists in "carrying out the will of God with joy." The will of God can come in silence and prayer. No matter what her schedule, she begins her day with contemplation, before assisting at Mass, and pauses again in the evening for an hour of prayer. This woman, honored for unexampled activity and achievement, is actually a contemplative in the world. The first step toward holiness is "the will to become holy . . . Everything depends on these words, I WILL or I WILL NOT." The turning of human wills to God is the sign of the coming of His kingdom. To everyone who would set her and her sisters apart in a separate category, too far from ordinary life for emulation, she says, "Holiness is not a luxury for the few, but the simple duty of all." She states publicly that she has need of confession like everyone else and that she depends on the mercy of God to forgive her faults. Mother Teresa serves as a living Beatitude, a reminder that only those who show mercy can obtain it. If there are those who might feel that they can cleanse their souls by donating to her work, they might ponder on her insistence on the inescapable, personal duty to serve Jesus, first within the family, then in near neighbors, and then in far neighbors in the world.

Mother Teresa sees meaning in the immensity of suffering that afflicts the human family, often the most innocent part of it. She has called the world "an open Calvary," identifying the suffering she sees with the redemptive suffering of Christ. Thus no suffering is meaningless. Of the sisters, whose work often involves willingly accepted suffering, she says, "Without our suffering, our work would be just social work, very good and helpful, but it would not be the work of Jesus Christ, not part of the redemption." Despite the evil and mercilessness of human beings toward each other, and despite what they may will to do against each other in the future, Mother Teresa is a person of hope. She shares that eschatological hope expressed by the English woman mystic, Julian of Norwich, that the worst, "the greatest harm," has already come upon mankind in the fall of man into sin, and that has already been remedied by the willing sacrifice of Christ.

To Mother Teresa, Christ is always present, either in "the other" whom she meets anywhere and everywhere, or in the Eucharist, the body and blood of the risen Christ. She couples the command of Jesus to feed the hungry with the fact that his flock can go to him to be fed at the altar. And as He has risen, so may all rise to where all hungers are satisfied.

In the face of a world wasting its resources on preparations for massive destruction, Mother Teresa has a twofold message of peace, the works of mercy—which are interrupted or reversed by war—and the conviction of the divine spirit in everyone including the enemy. At a meeting of world religions in Singapore, she stated, "All the works of love are works of peace. . . . We do not need bombs and guns; we need love and compassion." She posed the question to an interviewer, "If everyone could see the image of God in his neighbor, do you think we should still need tanks and generals?"

At the Nobel ceremony, the President of the Nobel Committee pointed to her witness to the inviolability and dignity of every person and asked if any project however principled or idealistic could be anything but a house of sand "unless the spirit of Mother Teresa inspires the builders and takes its dwelling in their building." There are certainly millions of people who want peace but are willing to expunge some part of the human family for a principled and idealistic cause. For

Mother Teresa the reverence for life is a seamless garment. In her Nobel acceptance speech, she spoke against the destruction of the unborn. It was near Christmas, and she did it in her own way.

"When the Virgin Mary," she said, "discovered that Jesus had come into her life, she went in haste to give that good news to Elizabeth. The child in the womb of Elizabeth leapt with joy. That little unborn child recognized the Prince of Peace." Nothing could be more logical than for Mother Teresa, who saw Jesus in "the other," to see him in the unborn, as John the Baptizer had done.

Even those who may not share all her beliefs see Mother Teresa and her work as a finger pointing to a merciful view of human life that might save a humanity threatened by thermonuclear cremation. Her peace message on the protection of all life, starting in the womb and englobing every member of the human family is one that goes counter to the laws of many nations and to all the arms stockpiles targeted on this or that segment of humankind. She lives a theology of peace needed at a historical moment when any resort to violence may result in apocalyptic and irreversible violence. Her message, the working out of which has given many a glimpse of the reign of God, is simply the utter inviolability of all human life and the need to nurture the least and the lost by the works of mercy—mercy being only love under the aspect of need, love going out to meet the needs of the person loved.

# THE CONTRIBUTORS

### JOHN DEEDY

Born in Worcester, Massachusetts, John Deedy holds
degrees from Holy Cross there and from Trinity College, Dublin. He was a reporter and correspondent for
daily newspapers in Worcester and Boston until 1951
when he entered religious journalism. He was editor of
the Worcester diocesan paper, the *Catholic Free Press*
in 1951–59 and the *Pittsburgh Catholic* in 1959–67.
He became managing editor of *Commonweal* in 1967,
a position he held until 1978 when he elected to enter
independent journalism, and wrote a column for that
journal. He has written or edited several books, has
contributed articles to the New York *Times*, *The Critic*,
*U. S. Catholic*, *The New Republic*, and other journals.
His most recent book is *Apologies, Good Friends . . . ,*
An Interim Biography of Daniel Berrigan, S.J.

### JOHN J. DELANEY

A native New Yorker, he was educated and has lived
all his life in New York. He has spent his entire career
in the book world, the past three decades and a half in
Catholic publishing. As editorial director of Doubleday's Catholic Division, he has been responsible for the
publication of Image Books and the Jerusalem Bible in
the United States and has published books by practi-

cally every important Catholic author of the past quarter of a century. He is coauthor of *Dictionary of Catholic Biography* and *A Guide to Catholic Reading,* editor of the Catholic Viewpoint and Catholic Perspective series, *A Woman Clothed with the Sun,* and *Saints for All Seasons,* has translated the seventeenth-century spiritual classic *The Practice of the Presence of God,* and is the author of *Dictionary of Saints.* He is the recipient of numerous literary awards, among them the Thomas More Medal and the Campion Award, and an honorary doctorate from Rosary College.

### EILEEN EGAN

Born in Pontypridd, Wales, of Irish parents, she was educated at Hunter College and Mt. St. Scholastica College and then became associated with Catholic Relief Services. Her work with refugees and the displaced brought her into contact with Mother Teresa in Calcutta in 1955. She visited Calcutta several times after that and became Mother Teresa's travel companion on trips to Europe and Latin America. She is Vice-Chairman of the International Co-Workers of Mother Teresa, a lay group with branches in a dozen countries, formed to aid Mother Teresa in her work. She is an associate editor of the *Catholic Worker,* co-founder of the United States branch of Pax Christi and its UN representative, and was a Holy See delegate member to the 33rd session of the UN General Assembly. She is author of *Works of Peace* and *Strangers and Pilgrims,* a history of Catholic Relief Services, articles in *America, Commonweal,* and *Worldview,* among others, and has contributed to several book collections. She has received honorary degrees from Holy Cross College and Benedictine College, has received the Grand Merit Cross from West Germany, and has been decorated for her relief work by France. She is presently working on a full length biography of Mother Teresa.

## JOHN MCCAFFERY

A native of Scotland, he was educated at St. Aloysius College there, Blairs College in Aberdeen, and Scots College in Rome. He received his M.A. from the University of Glasgow and his Ph.D. from the Gregorian in Rome, and then spent seven years as an English lecturer at Genoa University and Italian correspondent for several English newspapers. During World War II he was chief representative of SOE, the British counterpart of the American OSS, operating from Berne in organizing and supporting European Resistance movements. He was invested with the rank of Grand Officer in the Order of Saints Maurice and Lazarus, the oldest military order in the world, by King Umberto, and was made Freeman of the city of Milan by the Republican government that succeeded Umberto for services rendered to the Italian Resistance during the war. After the war he engaged in banking and helped form a European anti-Communist bulwark from various national leaders of Resistance movements with whom he had worked during the war. He retired to County Donegal in Ireland a dozen years ago to breed Connemara ponies; until his death in early 1981, he continued to write, lecture, and broadcast. A friend and admirer of Padre Pio, he is the author of the highly acclaimed *Tales of Padre Pio*.

## GARY MACEOIN

Born in Sligo, Ireland, he was educated at the University of London and the National University of Ireland, was admitted to the Dublin bar in 1943, and received his Ph.D. from the National University of Ireland in

1951. He has traveled widely all over the world and is versed in ten languages. He has taught at several universities, has lectured at more than fifty universities and colleges in the United States and Canada, and is regarded as an outstanding authority on contemporary Latin America. He has written scores of magazine articles, is the author of a dozen books, makes frequent TV appearances, and has received numerous awards. An American citizen since 1958, he lives with his wife in Tucson, Arizona, but still travels extensively, lecturing on matters dealing with world development, Latin America, and the Church.

### WILLIAM D. MILLER

Born in Jacksonville, Florida, William Miller received his B.A. from the University of Florida, his M.A. from Duke University, and his Ph.D. from the University of North Carolina. He has been a teacher for more than three decades beginning at Memphis State University, then at Florida State University, and now at Marquette. He was married in 1944, has had eight children, and in 1954 the whole family became Catholic. He has written the history of the Catholic Worker movement in *A Harsh and Dreadful Love* and will soon publish a full length biography of Dorothy Day. In a note about the Catholic religion he embraced he said: "I found in the Catholic Church an intellectual dimension that transcended all my liberal and radical positions and seemed to answer in a way more profoundly than any other I knew about, the central questions relating to existence."

### PHILIP SCHARPER

Philip Scharper is Editor in Chief of Orbis Books and one of the most distinguished Catholic laymen in the

United States. A native of Baltimore, he received his
B.A. from Woodstock, his M.A. in English from Fordham and in education from Georgetown, as well as a
licentiate in philosophy from Georgetown. He has
taught English at Xavier and Fordham universities,
was associate editor of *Commonweal* in 1955–57, and
Editor in Chief of Sheed & Ward, Inc. from 1957 to
1970 when he left to go to Orbis Books. He has written
articles for such magazines as *Harper's*, *Thought*,
*Christian Century* and *The Critic*, and has contributed
to numerous book collections. He is the author of *Meet
the American Catholic* and has written the scripts for
some thirty religious TV programs produced by NBC,
CBS, and ABC, many of which received awards from
all over the world. He has served on numerous commit-
tees and Vatican commissions, is a sought after lecturer, and has addressed national conventions of Catholic, Protestant, and interfaith groups. He has received
honorary doctorates from six universities and is the recipient of numerous awards including the Edith Stein
Award.

### EDWARD S. STANTON

Edward Stanton is a Jesuit priest who has taught theology at Holy Cross College and is presently a member
of the Theology Department at Boston College. He met
Father John LaFarge during the summer of 1963 when
he was serving as an editor on the staff of *America* in
New York and was most impressed by his holiness—so
much so that when he was asked to select his thesis for
his doctoral dissertation at the University of Ottawa in
the early seventies, he chose as the subject of his thesis
Father LaFarge's contribution to the American Church
in the areas of racial and ecumenical understanding.
With this background, he was the ideal person to do
the article in this book on John LaFarge.

## NAOMI BURTON STONE

Born in Woking, England, Naomi Burton joined the prestigious literary agency Curtis Brown, Ltd., in London after a year of secretarial school. She came to New York in 1939 and eventually became head of the Curtis Brown Book Department here, handling many well-known literary figures, among them Thomas Merton. She became an American citizen in 1945, married Melville Stone in 1951, and in 1955 became a Catholic. After twenty years with Curtis Brown, she joined Doubleday & Company, Inc., in 1959 as a senior editor; in 1969 she left Doubleday to take an editorial post with the McCall Book Company. Since 1964, when her autobiography *More Than Sentinels* was published, she has lived with her husband at York, Maine, where she is active in CCD work. She lectures and gives courses on religion, is active in liturgical affairs and has served on the board of the Liturgical Conference, and writes a weekly column for *Church World*, Maine's diocesan paper. She is one of the three trustees of Thomas Merton's literary estate, was a close friend and confidante of the Trappist monk before his tragic death in 1968, and is active in promoting further interest in his life and work.